History of the Farmstead

By the same author

AGRICULTURAL BUILDINGS—PLANNING & ALLIED CONTROLS,
Capital Planning Information, Edinburgh
(Ed.) COLESHILL MODEL FARM—PAST, PRESENT & FUTURE,
Architects in Agriculture Group, RIBA, London
FARM BUILDINGS, Vol. 1, Crosby Lockwood;
Vol. 2, Crosby Lockwood Staples
MODERN AGRICULTURE AND RURAL PLANNING, Architectural Press
PLANNING FARM BUILDINGS, Farm Buildings Information Centre,
National Agricultural Centre

By J. B. Weller and U. Chiappini
COSTRUZIONI AGRICOLE E ZOOTECHNICHE, Edagricole

By J. B. Weller and A. Coleman, G. Moss (& others)
LAND USE PERSPECTIVES, Land Decade Educational Council, London

By J. B. Weller and S. Willetts
FARM WASTES MANAGEMENT, Crosby Lockwood Staples

Treading out the Grain by Jéan-Leon Gerôme. From the collection of paintings at the Mathaf Gallery, 24 Motcomb Street, London SW1.

History of the Farmstead

THE DEVELOPMENT OF ENERGY SOURCES

John Weller

faber and faber

First published in 1982
by Faber and Faber Limited
3 Queen Square London WC1
Printed in Great Britain by
Fakenham Press Limited, Fakenham, Norfolk
All rights reserved

© John Weller, 1982

To Ann

British Library Cataloguing in Publication Data

Weller, John
    History of the farmstead: the development
        of energy sources
    1. Farms—History   2. Power resources—History
    3. Farm equipment—History
    I. Title
    631.3'71   S675

    ISBN 0–571–11804–6
    LSBN 0–571–11805–4 Paperback

Contents

4   *Contents*

Illustrations

12   Illustrations

Introduction

Our ancestors, unlike the ape, were carnivores. For hundreds of millennia early man hunted, killed and ate. He also picked fruits from the primeval forests through which he passed. He was a nomad. Slowly, he learnt the control of fire, the technique of cooking. The roots of civilization began when man started to herd and domesticate animals as stock and, later, to cultivate and harvest plants as crops. But around ten thousand years ago, families began to settle, to create steadings and to become farmers.

Settlement is essential for agriculture: productivity is the essence of civilization. To garner crops, you must plough, cultivate and sow. You must follow the seasons. You do not abandon fertile land wrested from the forest. Year follows year and the family builds a defensible steading. Each man, aided by his wife, produces enough for one family, perhaps providing food for five or six people. A village becomes practical only when one man can feed ten people. Then, perhaps, someone can become a craftsman. When agriculture flourishes from fertile soils, each farmer will support two families and then craftsmen, priests and artists flourish and civilizations are born.

Civilization, as we understand the term, is six millennia old, though some earlier towns did exist. A town is a place of commerce and of government. Later, it became a centre for industry and for arts. The emerging great towns of the Greek and Roman empires were possible only because the farmer could feed at least two or three families, that is perhaps a ratio of one to twenty-five people. For two millennia, from 500 BC to AD 1500, this ratio hardly changed. The emergence of cities, like London, was the exception to the small market towns set in an agrarian landscape.

Within the last three centuries, even less, there have been two great agricultural revolutions which have changed the world. The first was that of the eighteenth century. The innovation of controlled rotation of crops, including root vegetables, backed by improvements in field equipment made human survival easier. It became practical to maintain livestock through the long European winters. Autumn slaughtering and salting down of valuable stock reduced the potential for herds and flocks of any great size. It meant that famine was a reality following the failure of one harvest. Improvements in field management and in fodder conservation reduced the risk of failure and, in any case, better transport made local failure less of a disaster. The names of Jethro Tull with his seed-drill, of James Arbuthnot with his mould-board plough, and of 'Turnip' Townshend with his four-year rotations have become the symbols of a new age. Without them, and others of illustrious name among the eighteenth-century improvers, there could have been no Industrial Revolution.

The first agricultural revolution increased the farmers' potential to feed an expanding urban population. It became possible for one farmer to support thirty people. Thus for every agricultural family unit, together with the service industries for a rural community, at least one or perhaps two industrial and urban families could be maintained. This became more possible with a feed-back of technology from the town to the farm. During the nineteenth century, there was increased awareness that man had to harness new sources of power, initially that of steam, to increase the productivity of his labours. There was a zenith in the balance of European, particularly English, towns and country between 1865 and 1875. Each adult farm-worker, backed as he was by a wealth of technical innovation, was able to feed some thirty-five people.

The abundance of American prairie food entered Europe and, by 1880, cheap imported wheat and chilled meat devastated English agriculture which went into a decline for fifty years. The First World War gave the incentive to support agriculture as a national industry but the second agricultural revolution, based on electrical and diesel power, had a slow start. Tractors, combine harvesters and vacuum milking began to show their potential in the 1930s. The Second World War heightened awareness that 'island' communities, enclosed by sea or by hostile neighbours, must seek self-sufficiency in food production. The second agricultural revolution, in broad terms, took place within the four decades from 1940. Each decade focused on one significant innovation, each transforming food production. In reality, of course, these innovations both overlap and impinge on each other.

The greatest impact of the 1940s was from the power of the tractor, with all its attachments, and from the harvester. This was a mechanical revolution which had had its beginnings in Edwardian times. Essentially, it transformed field-work, later leading to the removal of hedges and to the amalgamation of farms as machines became more powerful. The tractor and the stationary engine had a profound effect on farm buildings. The forearm to a tractor and the power-take-off from a tractor made light of much work around the farmstead. Humping materials on a man's back began to retire into history and the pitchfork into museums. This period coincided with the post-war zeal for social change. The Agriculture Act of 1947 gave an organizational base for farm improvement with its now hallowed concept of 'promoting and maintaining, by the provision of guaranteed markets and assured prices ... such part of the nation's food and other agricultural produce as in the national interest it is desirable to produce in the United Kingdom and of producing it at minimum prices consistent with proper remuneration and living conditions for farmers and workers in agriculture and at an adequate return on a capital invested in the industry'.

Electrical power transformed the steading in the 1950s. It is true that electricity on the farm gained credibility in the 1930s. However, overhead supply reached the majority of lowland farms only in the decade or so following the impetus of the 1947 Act that created agricultural support from an urban society. Power had two main effects. Crop drying or conditioning, particularly of grain, became a normal farm task and, with it, the capacity to mill and mix livestock fodder. Second, heat and ventilation to stock buildings became practical and with this the intensive housing of animals and, eventually, the factory farm which can be divorced from agricultural land like any other industry. These innovations have had far-reaching implications both for feeding an unprecedented world population expansion and also for the balance between country and town within the United Kingdom. It has also created a moral problem of attitudes to food production, particularly of livestock.

The 1960s were a period of technical consolidation within a managerial revolution. Farming lost some of its image as a 'way-of-life' within a craft mystique. It was shown to be an industry susceptible to the jargon of industry. End products could be planned to precise specifications within flow-line production. Intensive production relied on capital investment and contracted sales. The power of the open market began to wane. Lean content of fatstock was measured by ultrasonic scanners. Eggs flowed from hen to package on conveyors. Crops were grown without soil, hydroponically. Textured meat came from soya beans. But, above all, the cost accountant, work study and cash flow became the base from which building investment was made. Buildings became larger and less sympathetic as a contribution to the environment.

The 1970s, in retrospect, will probably be seen to be the age of electronics. Cows are milked and fed in quantities directly related to each other by a programme planner: the more milk comes out, the more feed drops from a dispenser. Farm records pass into a computer which presents an evaluation of what to grow when and where. Traditional enterprises may be dismissed from a farm; and personal judgement, like folklore, may become suspect as a basis for decision. Farming becomes a matter of records, book-keeping and bureaucracy. Buildings, squeezed by an economic recession, are of disproportionate cost. At the same time, their innate social problems as working and landscape environments begin to be taken more seriously than for a generation.

Throughout two centuries of revolutionary changes in farm building design, and to some extent throughout history, technical innovation has been focused on the elimination of manual work and on increased quality control over crops and stock. Building innovations, for the most part, reflect farm managerial changes. Most farm buildings are set within a functional tradition. Sometimes this merely reflects status in that their efficiency is exaggerated and materials and detail become, to more spartan eyes, extravagant. Style, even decorative features, are rare in farm buildings. Model farms which to some extent shadow the age in which they were built have existed throughout history, though particularly as part of the eighteenth-century awareness of landscape.

There is one matter, other than technical innovation, which separates our farm buildings from those of past generations. No longer is a farm building a fixture in the sense of having continuity. It is equipment which, like a tractor, has a short, depreciated life. Most modern farm buildings have an economic life of ten years. Technical and managerial change is so rapid that, today, a decade is a long time. This has made farm buildings shack-like, of low capital cost and, often, of poor performance. The attitudes of a throw-away society have pervaded the buildings of the last twenty years. An energy-conscious world may change this in the 1980s.

We have reached a stage when approximately two-thirds of the food eaten in Britain comes from our own agriculture. Equally, one farm-worker now can feed about a hundred people. In theory, with modern technology, we have not reached a limit in productivity per worker. However, there is an antithesis. Some believe it would be a healthier society if automation did not remove all contact with manual labour. Forecasts are difficult to make, but it seems likely that in many developed countries there will be three main types of farm.

For one type of farming the term 'agribusiness' was coined in the early 1960s. It related to financial control over the production, process-ing and distribution of food. This implied a growth in the scale of production and of business management in farming. Top managers could not be justified on a small farm. At the same time, with linked financial control, came vertical integration in the chain of command from field to supermarket. Many companies have an international base: the need for a new building on a farm can be determined in a boardroom across an ocean. The company farm—even perhaps nationalized farms—will remain with us. In many cases, farmland and, therefore, buildings become part of a financial portfolio within companies primarily unconcerned with food. At the same time, as far as most seers report, the family farm will continue. This is likely to be anything from 50 to 250 hectares in size. Some will be specialized and intensive units with factory-type buildings. Others, particularly in contoured terrain or marginal or upland areas, will look more like the popular image of the nineteenth-century countryside. Old buildings may be retained; stead-ings may still have courtyards. Recreational facilities and food produc-tion equally will be the family's objective. Third, and not dissimilar, will be the smaller farm, probably of up to 100 hectares, run with low inputs of fossil fuels, but using modern forms of natural and muscular energy—the alternative and intermediate technologies now being developed. Windmills, watermills, solar 'mills', of new forms, will be part of the steading. Horses, even oxen and donkeys, may once again be harnessed. In many cases, the steadings will be small communities, sharing facilities and working together. The Scottish clachan type of settlement (see Plate 11) may be reborn.

A comprehensive review of innovation in the farmstead, across several thousand years and in many countries, cannot be carried out in one small book. The subject is vast, but essentially it can be considered as a question of how energy has been harnessed to assist in the production and quality control of food. Energy, until the Industrial Revolution, was almost entirely equated with two sources—natural and muscular in origin. Natural sources gave primary power, as they will again, to work in farmsteads and buildings. They gave power by harnessing the natural energy of the sun, gravity, water and wind. These were augmented by sources of secondary power derived from the muscles of man and beast. Oxen, donkeys and horses, sometimes other animals, became the beasts of burden, but also man's helpmates and friends. Men who work with animals have a very special relationship, even an affinity of love, respect and thought.

Power, as we know it today is the release of energy from fossil fuels. Nuclear reactors, of course, now produce electricity which also reaches the farmstead. But the evolution of power has progressed through the use of warmed air, to steam, to gas, to diesel and to electricity.

Innovation on the farmstead, can be studied by looking at the development of primary, secondary and indirect sources of power. An understanding of the farmstead, however, does need to include reference to the basic customs and forms related to building. There is a difference between the co-operative and the family farm. The family may live under one roof with their stock, and most farmsteads are formed as courtyards to give protection. The modern farm, serving as a factory, is linear. A few, adopting a logical scheme in organization of work, are radial. Each makes a distinct contribution to the landscape. Many special types of building can be identified and could be the subject of separate studies. Two, only, have been examined in detail here, both of them for storage. The rick is crop storage without a building. The container is crop storage with a thin skin to hold it together.

Underlying all modern custom and form in relation to farm building has been the shift from traditional materials to the prefabricated, sometimes package-deal, construction. This change in construction technology and management has had—is having—a profound effect on the countryside. Old farm buildings, based on the timber truss, with narrow spans, thick walls and small doorways are being swept away to make room for modern factories.

Our generation still looks out, however, on a countryside which contains many farm steadings that are remarkably unchanged, but for minor adaptations, since the time they were built. We witness, as we travel, groups of buildings which reflect the technology and sociology of medieval, Georgian, Victorian and Edwardian farms. They represent an unbroken, historical record of 500 years of agrarian development. In some country estate offices are detailed records over two or three hundred years which identify what was built by whom and for what purpose. John Popham, preparing a thesis in 1972 at the Institute of Advanced Architectural Studies at York, examined the Birdsall Estate in North Yorkshire. When the open pastures were enclosed, Georgian steadings were built for the thirty tenanted farms. The Agent to the Estate wrote a report on each steading in 1865 prior to a modernization programme. Each Georgian layout was recorded. Again, in 1875, a further report was made to show the High Victorian improvements to those steadings which then remained almost unchanged, but for disrepair, for another century. A record of 200 years evolution from the original enclosures exists. Similar studies could be made on many another estate. It is almost too late. Traditional steadings are being demolished—or allowed to fall into ruin—all over the world as modern food production becomes an industrial process.

Industrial Archaeology evolved as a discipline during the 1950s and many books and reports are available on the subject. When R. A. Buchanan published his *Industrial Archaeology in Britain* in 1972 (Pelican), he stated that there were 'no comparable works on agriculture' as a source of reference. Brian Bracegirdle wrote an account of *The Archaeology of the Industrial Revolution* in 1973 (Heinemann). Though this included valuable references to the development of power for farm and industry, food production was not identified as a subject which demanded its own technology. Medieval archaeology, and that of other periods, is revealing new knowledge on steadings and their layout, but the County Series on Industrial Archaeology makes only random references to the development of farm technology.

Nigel Harvey, in 1970, published his bibliography *A History of Farm Buildings in England and Wales* (David & Charles). His work has to be the base for any further study and this book is indebted to his source material, but he reported of farm buildings that 'no general history of their development based on original research has so far appeared—this book merely seeks to summarise the information at present available'. The situation is not greatly changed today. Furthermore, old estates are often broken up and records dispersed; buildings are being destroyed and original fittings from many remaining buildings are discarded. Many lie lost in undergrowth; some become curios for the antique trade. Travelling in Scotland in 1962, to give but one example, I saw suspended from the ceiling in a cowshed rows of 'horn curlers' which fitted over Highland cattle whilst they slept to ensure that each pair of horns matched in graceful curves. They had been there for generations. They are unlikely to remain. A small detail, a curio of another age, will have been lost. This study will be of some value if it awakens a wider interest in recording the passing of the historic farm building and in conserving its best examples. Dr. Edward Peters began a movement in the 1970s to this end following his study of farms in lowland Staffordshire. Small interested groups do exist, but much still needs to be done.

Studies of vernacular buildings in Europe, and elsewhere, often record humble farmsteads as part of a wider study. In France, for example, the Musée National (of the arts and popular traditions—which we know as the folk arts) began a series in 1978 for each region of the country under the title *L'Architecture rurale française* which records, with measured drawings, many such buildings. But seldom are the techniques of food production and of mechanization taken into account. It is the building and not the process which is recorded. What is required, eventually, is the synthesis of vernacular building, industrial archaeology, and of agrarian social history within one comprehensive study.

This book is about the evolution of sources of power to assist the storage, processing and production of food within the farmstead. In agriculture, there is a close affinity both in management and in mechanization between land and buildings. Indeed, the Ministry of Agriculture has termed the latter as 'fixed equipment'. But to consider the farmstead only as a matter of equipment is to misunderstand its relationship to the rural environment. Much that is wrong about modern farm buildings stems from that error. Part One examines briefly some of the environmental influences on the evolution of the steading which arise from social need, from topography and from farm management. Part Four outlines, equally briefly, some of the influences which stem from building technology. Each of these discussions could form the basis of a book in its own right. However, the main theme of this book is the evolution of power sources. This has two main aspects. Part Two considers how primary and secondary sources of power have influenced the farmstead. Primary relates to natural energy and secondary to the use of muscle, whether of man or beast. Though natural energy has again become a focus of interest, the Industrial Revolution, which also embraced the industry of agriculture, was concerned with the development of indirect sources of power largely based on fossil fuels. Part Three considers the use of indirect forms of energy within the steading leading up to the application of automation.

The Writer's Influence

Agriculture has had many thinkers and prophets. The great Greek Stoic, Epictetus, saw clearly that the pursuit of agriculture as a business—and this is equally true today—could demean mankind: 'There is a great difference between other men's occupations and ours. A glance at theirs will make it clear to you. All day long they do nothing but calculate, contrive, consult how to wring profit out of foodstuffs, farms and the like. But I entreat you to understand what the administration and nature of the world is, and what place a being endowed with reason holds in it; to consider what you are as a person, and in what your good and evil consists.' A few centuries later, it was expressed more pithily that man should not live by bread alone. Farmers, throughout history, have gained a reputation for being hard business men. Many take pride in it. Nevertheless, there have been both great innovators and great visionaries and there are those who have seen how agriculture relates to wildlife and how both are embraced within nature. This relationship has been the subject of much poetry and painting.

Farm buildings, even farmsteads, have generated few great thinkers. The Romans, however, as original engineers, did give the matter particular attention. Technical writers, such as Vitruvius, Cato and Columella, gave advice both on the siting of farm buildings and on the organization required for different enterprises within them. For example, they made recommendations; as identified by K. D. White (see Bibliography):

1. Because of fire hazard, the bakehouse should be located outside the main farm building but in close proximity to it.
2. The corn mill should be located near the villa. Like the bakehouse its size was proportional to the number of labourers employed.
3. At least two ponds should be provided, one for geese and cattle, the other for soaking lupines.
4. Compost heaps must not be allowed to dry out, being placed to receive the house drains.
5. The threshing floor should be placed so as to be under the eye of the manager.
6. The drying floor must be an adjunct to the threshing floor so that half-threshed grain could be protected from a sudden shower.
7. Sheds should be provided to protect implements from rain, probably using a lean-to within the courtyard.

Marcus Vitruvius Pollio wrote his ten books on architecture, *De Architectura*, made famous during the Renaissance by Alberti, in the period 46–30 BC. Several chapters deal with farmstead design or with agricultural engineering (see page 98). Lucius Columella wrote his *Rules and Precepts of Husbandry* about a century later (see page 128).

Both influenced farm building design in the centuries of the Roman Empire.

Medieval monasteries were great centres for agricultural development and for carefully considered farmstead layouts, like that at St. Gall (Plate 8). The Elizabethans, too, were interested in good husbandry though they gave less impetus to farm building technology. However, the eighteenth-century agricultural revolution gave a new impetus to thinkers and designers for farm buildings. The prevailing standard of buildings was poor; with the exception of the great barns they were little more than hovels. The report by John Grey as late as 1843, in the *Journal of the Royal Agricultural Society of England*, under the title 'On Farm Buildings', summed up what must have been the norm throughout many centuries:

> No one can have travelled much in the rural districts of England, even in those which are comparatively well cultivated, without being struck, if he have any sense of neatness and order, with the ill-arranged and patch-work appearance of many of the farm buildings, which are often placed, in relation to their different parts, in utter defiance of the economy of labour in the case of the cattle; and, what is still worse, with little regard to the production and preservation of the manure, the dry parts of which may be seen exposed to the winds, and the liquid part carried off without being applied to any beneficial purpose. In some the practice still prevails—the unnatural practice, I must call it—of tying up cattle intended to be fattened for the market to stakes, from which they are never released till they are driven off to the butcher—denied all the time the natural use of their limbs, the choice of their position in lying down, and the means of varying the atmosphere in which they are confined—a matter in which cattle are peculiarly discriminating and sensitive. When, at length, set at liberty to perform a weary journey to their place of execution, they are seen suffering in their bodies from exposure, and in their limbs from the unwonted exertion of walking, with their feet bruised and swollen to such a degree that the hoofs sometimes come off altogether.

The modern outcry against crated and chained animals, for example by Ruth Harrison in *Animal Machines* published in 1964, reflects an age-old problem of husbandry.

It was against such standards witnessed by Grey that new thoughts on farmstead planning had begun to appear in the first half of the nineteenth century. The effect of the Board of Agriculture, created in 1793, with its unique county by county survey during the Napoleonic Wars, concentrated the mind of agriculturists—and of society in general—on the part farm buildings could contribute to a healthy agriculture. The reports, quoted elsewhere, of Arthur Young and William Marshall were invaluable. However, another of the same band of surveyors, I. Leatham, wrote *The General View of the Agriculture of the East Riding of Yorkshire* in 1794. He gave a clear direction about the layout for a courtyard farm:

> Farm offices, when properly built, should form a square; and all the offices should be placed as conveniently and as near each other as possible: the fold

yard should be in the centre; and the pump and watering trough should be near the back door (of the house) where the cattle should be watered, to prevent the loss of their dung. . . . the stackyard should adjoin the barn, to prevent waste by carrying the corn from a distance; and the granary should, if possible, be over the carriage-shed, or any other place where it can be built in a situation equally cool and airy, and not over a stable. (p. 27)

A group of writers came to the fore at the turn of the eighteenth century. In 1802, John Plaw wrote a treatise on *Rural Architecture*. But this concentrated on the design of farm houses and cottages. James Malton, a year later, wrote *An Essay on Rural Architecture*, again of a domestic nature. Similarly, Joseph Gandy published *The Rural Architect* in 1805 which also discussed dwellings. However, he did illustrate one Rural Institute for agriculture, botany, fossiology, hot house, farriery, mechanics, chemistry, and territorial affairs. This showed new ideas about agricultural education and its technical base. Nevertheless, it was not until 1845 that a Royal Charter was granted to the first 'Agricultural College for teaching the Science of Agriculture' at Cirencester. This followed a public meeting held the previous year when it was resolved: 'That it is expedient to provide an institution in which the rising generation of farmers may receive instruction at a moderate expense, in those sciences a knowledge of which is essential

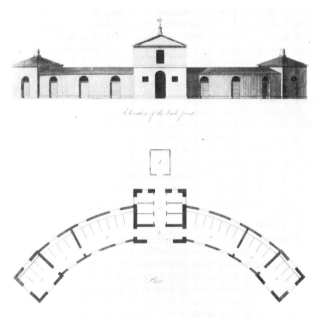

1. COW-BARN, Burn Hall, Co. Durham
1784

2. **GREAT BARN**, Holkham Hall, Norfolk
1790

to successful cultivation; and that a farm form part of such institution.'

Great innovators of the eighteenth century—such as Robert Bakewell (1725–95) of Dishley Grange in Leicestershire who did so much to improve livestock breeding and crop rotations, and who pleaded that experimental husbandry farms should be established—did not concentrate their energies on farm-building design. Some of the great period architects designed farm buildings in association with the great houses for which they were responsible. John Soane, for example, produced several Classical steadings such as that for a cow barn at Burn Hall, Co. Durham, designed in 1784 (Plate 1). Other architects, such as Robert Adams, Henry Holland, James and Samuel Wyatt, designed model estates. J. M. Robinson has produced a gazetteer of those built from 1730 to 1820. He records about seventy estates. Obviously, the model farm is a subject in its own right. Many were examples of landscape and architectural style. Most produced robust, healthy buildings for stock and crops. Not all introduced innovation in management or in mechanization. Samuel Wyatt's Great Barn at Holkham Hall for Thomas William Coke, Earl of Leicester, built in 1790, has been rightly admired for its grandeur and proportion (Plate 2). It gained Arthur Young's enthusiastic appreciation in 1792. The work of the Classical architects and, later, of the Romantics, such as Nash, has left a major contribution in the great parklands of Britain. A few, who were writers as well as architects, such as Nash, have influenced the cottages around the estates. The cottage ornée became a feature of rural Britain. But, the greater contribution came from two writers, Lugar and Loudon.

Richard Lugar published *The Country Gentleman's Architect* in 1807. This included a number of model designs for farm buildings and complemented the growing interest amongst the great estate owners to improve their agriculture, their country seat and their image.

John Claudius Loudon made a greater contribution to farmstead architecture than all the great period architects. This was because his writings had wide circulation and because he thought of the farmstead as part of and within a complete rural economy. Born in 1783, in Lanarkshire, as a young man he settled in 1807 at Wood Hall Farm, Pinner in Middlesex, after a few years in London. In his sixty years, dying in 1843, he wrote over thirty manuals, reports and text books. His earlier works, between 1804 and 1822 were mostly concerned with horticulture, hothouses and ornamental gardens—for which he became famous (Plate 67). He did write, in 1811, on *Designs for Laying Out Farms and Farmbuildings in the Scotch Style, Adapted to England*. He and many Scots who settled in East Anglia, particularly in the depression of the 1920s, introduced their native skills and became more successful farmers than the yeomen of Essex. In 1822 Loudon published his *Encyclopædia of Gardening* which had wide renown. This was followed by the *Encyclopædia of Agriculture* in 1825 and the *Encyclopædia of Plants* in 1829. But his greatest work, published in 1833 when he was forty, was his *Encyclopædia of Cottage, Farm and Villa Architecture and Furniture*. The first edition had 1138 pages in a comprehensive review of rural architecture, furnishing, style and taste. Six years later, so well received was his work, the second edition was increased to 1317 pages (Plate 3). The work was the twelfth in a series of encyclopaedias and dictionaries from the same publishers. It demonstrates the early nineteenth-century interest in the farm as part of the total environment. It had over 2000 engravings to illustrate 'the principles of architectural science and taste'. This mixture of an emerging technology and an appreciation of aesthetics makes the work almost unique. Certainly, never again has such a comprehensive work on farm, let alone rural, building embraced both science and appearance with such fine balance.

Loudon analysed the basic concept of the steading: 'The parts which compose a Farmery may be arranged under two heads, buildings and yards. The buildings may be classed as houses for lodging and feeding livestock; storehouses for produce and food; houses for preparing food, or carrying on in-door farmery operations; houses for portable machinery and implements; lodgings for single men and houses for married men. The yards are chiefly two; the cattle or dung yard, and the rick or stack yard: but in large establishments there are, besides these, the pig yard, the poultry yard, the carpenter and smith's yard, and some others, according to the kind of farm.' (p. 744)

Loudon's work was the springboard for an increased interest in farm technology throughout the middle years of the nineteenth century. At the time that J. Grey wrote his lament, in 1843, on the waste of resources on the average farm, especially of manure, another writer, F. Falkner, published *The Farmers Muck Manual* which aimed at: 'Being a concise

AN

ENCYCLOPÆDIA

OF

COTTAGE, FARM, AND VILLA

ARCHITECTURE

AND

FURNITURE;

CONTAINING

NUMEROUS DESIGNS FOR DWELLINGS,

FROM THE COTTAGE TO THE VILLA,

INCLUDING FARM HOUSES, FARMERIES, AND OTHER AGRICULTURAL BUILDINGS;

SEVERAL DESIGNS FOR

COUNTRY INNS, PUBLIC HOUSES, AND PAROCHIAL SCHOOLS;

WITH THE REQUISITE FITTINGS-UP, FIXTURES, AND FURNITURE;

AND

APPROPRIATE OFFICES, GARDENS, AND GARDEN SCENERY;

EACH DESIGN ACCOMPANIED BY

Analytical and Critical Remarks,

ILLUSTRATIVE OF

THE PRINCIPLES OF ARCHITECTURAL SCIENCE AND TASTE

ON WHICH IT IS COMPOSED.

By J. C. LOUDON, F.L.S. H.S. G.S. Z.S. &c.

CONDUCTOR OF THE ARCHITECTURAL MAGAZINE, ETC.

ILLUSTRATED BY

MORE THAN TWO THOUSAND ENGRAVINGS:

The Designs by upwards of fifty different Architects, Surveyors, Builders, Upholsterers, Cabinet-makers
Landscape-Gardeners, and others, of whom a List is given.

A NEW EDITION,

WITH NUMEROUS CORRECTIONS, AND WITH MANY OF THE PLATES RE-ENGRAVED.

LONDON:

LONGMAN, ORME, BROWN, GREEN, & LONGMANS,

AND SOLD BY

JOHN WEALE, AT THE ARCHITECTURAL LIBRARY, HIGH HOLBORN.

1839.

3. TITLE PAGE, J. C. Loudon, *Encyclopædia of Cottage, Farm and Villa Architecture and Furniture*, 2nd edition, 1839

Treatise on the Chemical Nature and Value of Animal and Vegetable Manures, founded from actual experiments on their application to various different Crops. With a brief Introduction, containing a scientific Account of Agricultural Chemistry, drawn up in a plain and simple manner for the information of the Practical Farmer.' Dr. Augustus Voelcker became the first professor of chemistry in 1849 at the newly founded Royal Agricultural College at Cirencester. In 1856, he published his famous account 'On the Composition of Farmyard Manure' in the *Journal of the Royal Agricultural Society of England*. Technology began, with manure, to be the basis for a new type of farm building and such work as Voelcker's started a revolution which made buildings part of the equipment for producing food. Loudon, and his emphasis on 'style and taste', began to be outdated. Nevertheless, there was another

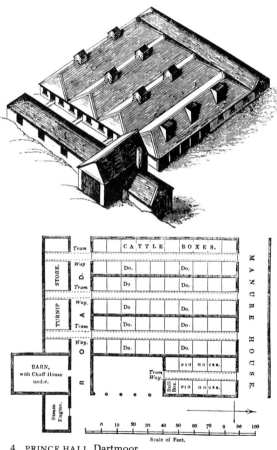

4. PRINCE HALL, Dartmoor
1848

5. EASTWOOD MANOR FARM, East Harptree, exterior, part of five-gabled end
1858

6. EASTWOOD MANOR FARM, interior, bullock yard as converted
to abreast parlour and collecting yard in the 1960s

great wave of model farm building during the zenith of agricultural
prosperity from 1850 to 1875, for example that for the Earl of Radnor at
Coleshill in 1852 (page 92). Many architects, surveyors and engineers
contributed to the new farmsteads of this period. Their history has yet to
be written.

At the outset, the Royal Agricultural Society of England did much to encourage new building. In its *Journal* of 1848, H. Tanner won a prize for his 'Report on the Farming of Devonshire', in which he described the homestead built for Mr. Fowler of Prince Hall, Dartmoor (Plate 4), designed by J. C. Morton—a well-known farm-building expert of Whitfield—specifically for the retention of manures and for utility in feeding. It was an early example of the totally enclosed structure as opposed to the more traditional courtyard layout. In 1858 another model farmstead was designed by Robert Smith, a land agent at Chew Magna in Somerset, for Eastwood Manor Farm in East Harptree (Plates 5 and 6). It was a completely roofed steading covering some 0.6 hectares. The building was designed around two large, indoor bullock yards, roofed in glass and corrugated iron, and complete with stabling for eight three-horse teams of carthorses, stallion boxes, carriage house and riding stables, as well as blacksmith's and carpenter's workshops. Such buildings were the forerunners of the improvements made throughout the next generation. After about 1875, the bankruptcy of British agriculture began and the days of great model farmsteads were almost over. However, engineering innovations in the development of power continued with steam, diesel and electricity during the next seventy years.

From 1865 to 1945, there were a number of books on farm-building design (see Bibliography), but these created no impact equal to that of Loudon's great work. In 1945, as one of a series of *Post-War Building Studies*, the government published its report *No. 17: Farm Buildings* (HMSO) and this had a profound effect—and later a restriction—on the rapid investment in farm buildings, which was given a boost by the Farm Improvement Scheme for grant aid in 1957.

In the United States, a number of technical, engineering-based standard works on farm buildings were published, most of which went through several revised editions:

1922   D. G. Carter, *Farm Buildings*, John Wiley
1941   J. C. Wooley, *Planning Farm Buildings*, McGraw-Hill
1950   H. J. Barre and L. L. Sammet, *Farm Structures*, John Wiley

In post-war Britain, a number of works cover different aspects of the subject:

1947   *New Ideas for Farm Buildings* (a report of a competition for designs), Farmer and Stockbreeder
1955   F. Henderson, *Build Your Own Farm Buildings*, Farming Press
1956   W. G. Benoy, *Farm Buildings and Conversions*, Crosby Lockwood
1965   D. H. Pasfield, *Farm Building Design and Construction*, Temple Press
1965   J. B. Weller, *Farm Buildings*, Vol. 1, Crosby Lockwood

1966   R. B. Sayce, *Farm Buildings*, Estates Gazette
1972   J. B. Weller, *Farm Buildings*, Vol. 2, Crosby Lockwood Staples
1977   J. B. Weller and S. Willetts, *Farm Wastes Management*, Crosby Lockwood Staples

Of all these works, only that teaching farmers how to 'build your own farm buildings' has gone into more than one edition. However, to keep abreast of rapidly changing technology and management, including the innovations in the use of power in the farmstead or farm building—our modern fixed equipment—a vast array of official and research-based reports need to be read. The subject is now too fragmented. It is hard to see how John Loudon would have coped. Epictetus, too, might have blanched at the economic pressures which have changed the countryside and turned farm buildings, too often, into buildings of cheap utility, sometimes being little more than shacks to 'wring profits out of foodstuffs'.

1   Custom and Form

Non-urban areas, the rural land of the world, can be classified in many different ways. The LAND Council, created in 1979, rightly makes a distinction between farmscape and wildscape. The former represents land used for man's bodily sustenance, through food production; the latter remains free of development, providing a habitat for wildlife and, also, space for man's spiritual needs. Coastal land, with its distinctive character, may belong to either or both classifications. In addition, there are two fringe areas, one between farmscape and wildscape and the other between farmscape and urban areas. Both fringes are a problem, socially and agriculturally.

The wildscape fringe includes, in particular, land which is worked with difficulty for food production. In many cases, it will be upland and hill farming areas, but it can be any lands with broken terrain, poor soils, or inhospitable climate. Farming can be tough and uneconomic. Isolation can be difficult for family life, made worse by low incomes. At times of food scarcity, governments tend to encourage fringe farming with subsidy and grants. Politics can change and, at other times, such subsistence farming may be abandoned and fringe areas revert to scrubland. Buildings are likely to be small scale, home-made and, often, shacklike as in the outback in all parts of the world. Today, serving tourism may prove a better base for economic habitation in such areas than food production. Equally, those who wish to opt out of urban life may well seek the rugged flavour of self-sufficiency in areas close to wildscape.

Areas of farmland close to conurbations have a particular problem. Pressure of need for recreation space spills out of the built-up area into the fields. Trespass, vandalism and theft are a malaise which can destroy the prosperity of such farmland, no matter how fertile it may be. As in medieval times, outlying buildings for storage and shelter are no longer practical—all needs to be under close control and supervision. Though twentieth-century farming does not need to have farmsteads, since power sources can be provided to outlying buildings, self-protection has become an urgent priority in building design. The areas where town and country, urban and rural life, meet are now called the rurban fringe. The selection of farm system, even of cropping, can be influenced by this factor.

All through history, the stealing of livestock from the ranch or field has been a commercial temptation. Rustling is a rural crime as rife today as at any period of history, especially close to fast motorways along which stock can disappear to far-away places almost instantly. All livestock, now, is a valuable commodity, worth the stealing. Diesel and petrol, too, have suddenly become a temptation for theft. Even standing crops can be harvested by the rustlers if supervision is not available and stored crops can be taken by any 'breaking-and-entering' thief unless well protected. Farm protection is likely to become a major issue in building design during the 1980s.

It is helpful to our understanding of the countryside today to have terms of land classification such as those of scape and fringe, but historically settlement began by the formation of self-sufficient communities. Each community retained within its control the four resources essential for freedom—food, water, fuel and materials. This did not prevent trade. But, at its roots, the power of the community lay in its control of resources. And, indeed, land in all rural areas was used to produce these resources. The 'farmer' might well be the provider of food, water, fuel and materials, the latter being both for building and for artefacts and chattels. Roman senators, mostly influential landowners and farmers, were men with precise standards of status. They could not be tradesmen or professional men. They could not be architects and engineers selling their skills. But they could be brick-makers and timber-merchants, since the produce of clay and of wood was seen as equal to that of grain, the rightful use of land resources which any landowner or farmer should undertake.

It is understandable that the origins of farm-building design should lie, as with all rural building, within what we call today the vernacular tradition. Perhaps, for the great monastic steadings for example, stone might be imported into clay regions or oak to where timber was scarce. But the tradition of buildings, as of speech, within the evolution of farming was of the vernacular. There was little structural or material distinction between byre, cottage or church. This homogeneity of buildings within a region, and between the buildings and the land, now gives us delight since, so often, our modern settlement has no roots in its locality. We have, in building terms, become the faceless ones.

This book is not a study of the vernacular tradition, since vernacular building has been well studied elsewhere. It is more an examination of the functional tradition. This was a phrase coined by J. M. Richards in his book of that title (Architectural Press, 1958). Simple engineered structures, such as for farms, mills, bridges and workshops, have a direct honesty in their relation between function and form. In the past, because materials used had the same limitations as for other vernacular buildings, the appearance of the buildings often had a rugged simplicity, sometimes grandeur, which delights the eye. There is a romantic link between the machinery used in the buildings and the structures which housed them. Equally, there are reasons, discussed briefly at the end of this book, why this quality has been largely lost to modern farm-building design.

The intention of this study is not to give a detailed account of the functional tradition so that the form, in terms of silhouette, mass and composition, can be analysed for mills, oasts, cotes, barns, byres and all the other basic and particular functional requirements of farm building. Essentially, the task is to examine how the evolution of power sources has influenced the functional tradition and has perhaps to some extent reacted to the vernacular tradition.

There are three types of farm enclosure of space according to the most basic functional analysis. These I discussed fully in my book on the design of modern *Farm Buildings* (Crosby Lockwood, 1965, p. 51):

> The basic function of any farm activity requiring the enclosure of a building is either for storage, for processing or for converting coarse foods. Each of these activities is performed within a defined space and such a space may form a complete building, a number of buildings being required to form the layout of an enterprise. However, the space required for an activity may form only a part of one building, the complete building being composed of a number of inter-related spaces.
>
> Storage buildings: are designed to maintain foods, materials or equipment in a satisfactory and convenient state, without changing the condition of the stored commodity. Storage is a subsidiary activity to those of processing and of converting coarse foods. Storage may be required prior to commodities being used in the buildings or in the fields, or prior to their sale from the farm.
>
> Processing buildings: are designed for foods or materials on the farm, in order to improve their quality or to change their physical state, either prior to their use on the farm or their sale from the farm.
>
> Production buildings: are designed to convert coarse foods, including grass and grass products, roots, grain and skim milk, into flesh or dairy products. Though the techniques of livestock fattening and of milk production are related principally to the food conversion ratio between the coarse foods and those for human consumption, there are numerous methods of obtaining this transformation.

The form of all three types of building—storage, processing, or production—will relate directly to the type of power and its source used within them. These are discussed in three broad groups depending on whether the source of the power comes from natural energy, muscular effort, or thirdly, from indirect power and fossil fuels. However, first it is desirable to outline some of the social factors which influence the type of steading created to serve a farm.

There are three main types of farmer in terms of land tenure. The breakdown of the feudal system led to the evolution of the yeoman farmer, especially in England, noted as a particularly independent and individual type of person. The yeoman was the forerunner of the owner-occupier as we know him today. In many cases, the same family still farms the land acquired following the Black Death when feudalism declined. Second, the great manors and monasteries let many of their farms to tenants. There has always been a race of non-land-owning farmers, some of whose families have worked the same land for genera-tions. There is an affinity of spirit between the yeoman and the tenant in traditional practice. A tenancy is likely to be held on a full repairing lease and, therefore, there is an incentive, as with an owner-occupier, to keep the land and its buildings 'in good heart'. Long-established land-lord–tenant relationships, too, can represent a close affinity of objec-tive. According to traditional practice, the buildings were erected so as to be passed down to succeeding generations. At the beginning of this century about four farms in five were tenanted from private landlords or from the great institutions such as the church, the universities, or the hospitals. Today, a reversal of social objectives has reduced the pro-portion to a little over two farms in five. The growth of owner-occupation and soon, possibly, of fragmentation of estates into smaller units, reflects changes in fiscal and taxation methods.

Co-operative farming and the third type of farmer have a particular niche in agrarian and social history. Bands of men have always wanted to work the land for the common good of their group and for social harmony in shared work. This has been so in the case of the monas-teries, of the communes and of the kibbutzim. But the high cost of equipping land with modern machinery has also influenced private land-owners to share their tackle within co-operatives. This can lead to particular types of farm layout and landscape.

Permutations of layout are infinite, yet basically of four main types: 1. the longhouse—the house and farmstead under one ridge—has had its own evolution as a form of family farm and it can be seen in many parts of the world. 2. The courtyard farm is most associated with lowland, mixed agriculture. It has distinctive characteristics which set it apart from the longhouse. 3. In contrast, though linear layouts of farm buildings have always existed, they are the hallmark of the modern, mechanized farm where handling of materials is the crux of the whole farm operation and management. 4. The efficiency of the radial plan has attracted a few devotees during the last few hundred years. However, such patterns are a rare feature in the landscape.

Though the rick yard is considered to be a traditional part of the farmstead, its history lasted only from about 1800 to 1950. In popular imagination, the courtyard and adjacent rick yard are the embodiment of a proper steading. Yet both patterns now belong to history, as much as the longhouse. Modern agriculture is evolving in other directions and the form of farm buildings is closer to the factory than to the dwelling.

Considering their basic form, there are three main types of modern farm building. First, there is the container which can be either a cylin-der or a box. Second, there are long, low, insulated sheds for livestock where minimum volume is desirable and linearity essential for the handling of materials. Third, there are the wide-span, high-portal framed enclosures, where the main requirement is a cheap umbrella to permit tractor and attachments to manoeuvre. Of course, there are other variants and specialist buildings, but the form of most modern buildings will be of one of these three basic variations.

Yeoman or Tenant

The yeoman farmer is part of the folklore of England. He provides one of the main distinctions between English and European history. Chaucer witnessed how manorial lords began to transmute the requirement on the serf to work his land on a rota service to one of a cash payment. Many of the new freemen founded the class of yeoman farmer. Some of them still worked their former lord's demesne, as tenants instead of bondmen. Others acquired wasted land or strips abandoned when the population was halved by the Black Death. New small farms were created and their owners learnt independence and self-reliant skills. Other yeomen became middlemen, traders, or retainers and left the land. But out of the yeoman class came the great bowmen of the Hundred Years' War, the hearty beef-eating farmers of the eighteenth century and, eventually, the middle class of rural society—that is, not the landed gentry, with great estates and court responsibilities, and not the landless, paid workers, who eventually left the countryside and moved into the urban factories of the nineteenth century.

Farm buildings for the yeoman stock have a distinctive character. First, they are practical. Money was never spent on them for effect. Second, the steading was the family's home and they respected quality and stability. Their buildings were well constructed and they had pride in their practical and ordered quality of design. The buildings contributed to the quality of the landscape. Third, their long history of use showed clearly in a process of adaptation and change within and around the buildings. Few farmsteads remained pure to one generation. They reflected generations which knew poverty as well as those which prospered. Today, they often reflect, too, a capacity for 'do-it-yourself' building which, though not always pleasant in the landscape, is part of this independence of tradition.

The tenant farmer has a different tradition of building. The landlord normally provides the structure—that is the main enclosure of space—which is leased with the farm and is taken into account in assessing the rent. But the tenant is responsible for equipping the building, and this can include partition walls as well as portable machinery. The landlord is likely to want to provide enclosure to serve a succession of tenancies. He may well have an objective different from that of the tenant who wishes to have a building suitable for one commodity. This division of responsibility may be reflected in the building performance as well as in its appearance.

The family farm, evolved by the yeoman, is likely to be self-contained. Landlords, too, may have relatively localized ownership of land to let. But the great estates, containing many tenanted farms, can influence the building tradition of vast tracts of countryside. There have been many lords who have boasted they could travel across their county from end to end without leaving their own land. Their land management is likely to be vested in a bailiff, factor or surveyor. The responsibility for investing in new buildings, both for dwelling and for farm purposes, is therefore centralized. The incentive to invest may well reflect a period of prosperity. In such cases, there will be a hallmark of design standards throughout the estate. It can be fascinating to observe this characteristic and the continuity of ownership across many parishes.

The great landlords may also have status as a motive for building. Model farms, especially those of the seventeenth and eighteenth centuries, provide a distinctive feature in the landscapes. But such buildings are seldom architectural conceits.

Investment in the productiveness of farmland has been a concern of the great landowners. Many have taken interest in new technologies and much of the context of this study about power sources reflects their readiness to take risks, to experiment and to improve. Thus many of the model farms are witnesses to the most advanced technology of their time.

The modern world is different. Owner-occupiers are on the increase as taxation policy splits up traditional estates. But owners are uncertain about the perpetuation of family inheritance and building becomes more makeshift. Tenants in Britain have now acquired the right to pass their tenancy to their children, so many owner-occupiers have made their sons their tenants.

Estate ownership has changed its character. Its focus is no longer towards the creation of a dynasty. Land ownership can be a hedge against inflation since land values tend to rise faster than inflation itself. This means land is bought and sold like stocks and shares. Continuity in farm management is disrupted and short term. The fertility of land and the quality of buildings can be neglected and assets stripped for short-term profit. Luckily, though this does happen, it has not been prevalent.

Land-tenure analysis is not the purpose of this book. However, in examining the evolution of building technology and mechanization, it is important to remember that there is another, and major, influence at work apart from the absolute desire for technical progress.

7. OPEN STRIP FIELDS, Laxton, Nottinghamshire
1947

The Co-operative Farm

Community farming, organized for the common good, has taken many
forms. It tends to create a distinctive landscape, sometimes requiring
special types of building. In the feudal system of land ownership, the
serfs farmed the demesne of the lord of the manor. The villein also had
his own strips of land to cultivate. 'Open field' land management was
established in the time of the Saxons and it was a widespread practice
south of the Yorkshire Wolds. Usually each village had three unen-
closed fields, one of which in rotation would be fallow. In addition,
there was often common land, where the rights of grazing and fuelling
belonged to the community. The villeins had specific duties of work for
their lord but in time these were commuted for a fee. The system began
finally to disintegrate following the Black Death of 1348. Chaucer in his
Canterbury Tales wrote of the emergence of a new society. The lord of
the manor began either to hire labour or to lease his farmland to those
who eventually became the yeomen of the Plantagenets. Strip cultivations, divided amongst many sons, were fragmented eventually to a
level of inefficient cultivation. By degrees, the richer men bought out
the poorer and separate fields emerged which, at the time of the
eighteenth-century enclosures, almost eliminated the old, open-field
landscape. One of the few to survive, and now protected as a monument, was the famous open-field system at Laxton in Nottinghamshire
(Plate 7). Originally the system worked well. Each field was managed by

the community for its own good within a web of legal constraints. The rotation of use was decided by the manor court and each man was expected to maintain a reasonable standard of cultivation without nuisance to his neighbours. Each strip was one chain wide by one furrow long (22×220 yards) which became known as the furlong. At Laxton, there were ten furlongs between the village and the surrounding forest. Between each furlong would be a narrow access turf-track. Each villein was granted equal strips of good and bad land. Buildings to hold the produce were the responsibility of each man at his own cottage. Usually there was little enough to store to last a long winter.

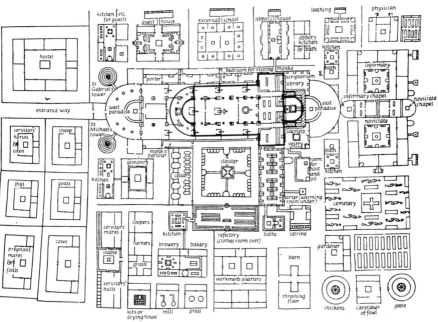

8. **ABBEY CO-OPERATIVE FARM**, Benedictine Monastery, St. Gall, Switzerland c. AD 830

In the monastery, the religious community worked as a team, each with his specialist task, according to his talents (Plate 8). Many of the abbeys were famous for their farming skills and much innovation stemmed from their work. The idealized layout for a Benedictine abbey (Plate 8), redrawn from the original of about AD 830, reflects the order and organized work particular to their beliefs. Around the great abbey would be the buildings provided for worship, teaching and dwelling. To one side, there were individual courts for oxen, sheep, pigs, goats, cows, and pregnant mares and foals. The chickens and geese had their

9.   GREAT COXWELL TITHE BARN, Berkshire, exterior
Mid-13th century

own compounds under their own caretaker. There were also special buildings for the barn and its threshing-floor, for the kiln, mill and press, as well as for the processing of food, baking, brewing and other kitchen work.

Under early laws, the great abbeys also collected a tithe of all produce from all tenant farmers of their many estates. Equally, the manors levied their tithes—that is a tenth of produce. All this 'collective' harvest had to be stored. In the case of grain, this created the need for the tithe barns to store the harvested sheaves. Some barns were of giant proportions and became a principal landscape feature. Tisbury tithe barn is described later (see Plate 101). The Great Coxwell tithe barn (Plates 9 and 10) was built in the mid-thirteenth century for the lands belonging to the Cistercian abbey of Beaulieu, in Hampshire. It was constructed with ashlar buttresses between Cotswold random stone, with a Cotswold stone-slated roof. It was some 46 metres in length and 14 metres to the ridge. Tithes were commuted by the Act of 1836 into a rent-charge and only recently have been abolished. The grievance against tithe laws were a major source of agricultural discontent. In principle, tithes were collected from the fortunate—those who were able to grow food because they had skill and access to land—and were then distributed to the poor via the monastic largesse to those who sought help. Thus, the tithe barn was a great co-operative store.

10. GREAT COXWELL TITHE BARN, interior

11. AUCHINDRAIN CLACHAN, Argyll, view from northern slopes 1963

12. AUCHINDRAIN CLACHAN, Argyll, view from south-east slopes (see also Plate 19)

Community living had many different forms, as it has today. The remote villages always had to work as a team. In Scotland, the clachan was a particular type of settlement: that at Auchindrain (Plates 11 and 12) was an eighteenth-century settlement held as a multiple tenancy from the dukes of Argyll. The last tenant quit in 1963. In its nineteenth-century prosperity, there had been some twenty principal buildings, including main barns, stock buildings and cottages. The clachan is now being restored as an open-air museum, to demonstrate the structure of a community which rented and worked a farming settlement under one

13. MODEL OF DAIRY UNIT, Dedelow, near Prenzlau, East Germany
1960s

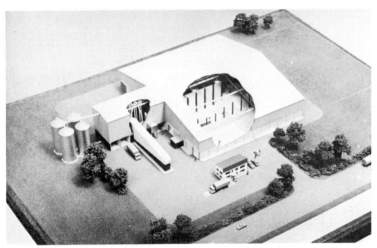

14. MODEL OF CENTRALIZED GRAIN STORE
1973

corporate management. To some extent, modern communist countries work with similar settlement patterns. The Chinese communes work with five to ten brigades, each with production teams of twenty to a hundred families working shared land with common equipment and service buildings. In Europe, centralized farms are built on a grand scale. A dairy unit in East Germany was planned in the 1960s for over 1000 cows, with covered yards, tower silos and open silage clamps (Plate 13). To the north, two storage tanks and pump house received all the effluent until it could be spread on the land.

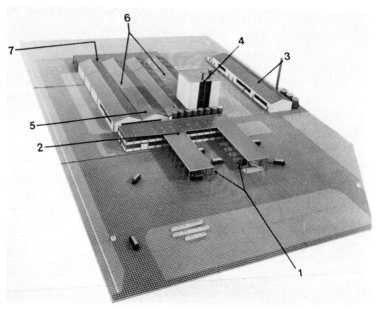

15. MODEL OF ALFRETON CREAMERY, Derbyshire
1970
1. automated bulk milk reception; 2. central control unit;
3. services; 4. spray drying tower;
5. cream processing and continuous butter churning;
6. butter and milk-powder stores; 7. dispatch

Centralized, co-operative-owned farm buildings are not unique to communist countries. Big co-operative grain silos have been a feature of France and the United States since the 1930s. In England, each farmer had been encouraged to have his own small store to hold his own produce. This has many disadvantages. In the early 1970s, Agricultural Co-operation and Marketing Services promoted a standard-unit grain store of about 15,000-tonne capacity. This would take corn from some 2500 hectares, probably within a ten-mile radius.

The demarcation between food production and processing cannot be clear-cut especially when ventures are owned co-operatively. In communist countries, both stages are owned by the state. In England, the state only owns directly some research and educational farms. But, since the days of the Board of Agriculture, the state has been partially involved in processing and marketing and, through advisory services, in production. The marketing boards were established in the 1930s for hops, milk, pigs and potatoes. The Milk Marketing Board, in particular, has achieved world renown for organizing milk from farm to doorstep. Milk has by-products in butter and skim milk powder. One of the most advanced factories was established for this purpose by the Board in 1970 on a five-hectare site (Plate 15). To some extent, this is a form of quasi-co-operative processing. It is a long way from the private farm dairy (see Plate 76). But its existence, with its contracts for milk production, does affect the size and layout of modern farms. The monthly milk cheque has been an incentive towards more efficient and larger dairy cattle units. Centralized units, some based on farmer co-operation, will become a feature of the countryside, making more efficient use of power in conditioning and processing food.

The Longhouse

Throughout most of history, and in most parts of the world, the family has been the unit working most farms. There has been a long tradition whereby the family and their livestock and storage have been housed under one long roof. It is a particular type of layout to be found in many different countries.

The origins of the tradition were illustrated in 1973 in *Man Made the Land*. A pre-Norman house at Wharram Percy, a now deserted village in Yorkshire, has been excavated by Dr. June Sheppard. The excavations revealed the stone foundations of the house showing a layout common over many centuries. The sketch is a reconstruction from the evidence (Plate 16). The house would have had a rough, simple timber frame, complete with wattle and daub panels and a straw roof. Oxen and sheep would be penned, but chickens would be loose. There would be space for general storage and for fuel. Living space would be in an open plan and around a central hearth, with its smoke hole in the roof above.

16. RECONSTRUCTION OF LONGHOUSE, Wharram Percy, North Yorkshire

17. WEST NEW HOUSE, Bishopdale, North Yorkshire
1635

There were variations to the plan form, especially when the family
had servants to assist on the farm. In larger types of longhouse, the stalls
for oxen and for cows would face each other across a wide threshing-
floor. Above the stalls would be dormitories, one for menfolk and one
for womenfolk. Set apart at one end of the longhouse would be the
family space around the cooking hearth. At the other end would be the
main-entrance barn doors. Entrance to see the head of the household
would be across the threshing-floor (later corrupted as the threshold to
the doorway).

The traditional form of the longhouse continued into the seventeenth
century and was particularly common in upland, stone areas. West New
House was rebuilt in 1635 (Plate 17). It is typical of the uplands, since
farms were small and a longhouse suited the contours. As the centuries
passed, it became more civilized to keep the building in three compartments, divided by cross-walls, to provide quarters for the family, the
livestock and the main storage barn. West New House has a roof of more
than 30 metres in length. The quarry for the building is to be seen
behind it.

Some longhouses have a specialist function. Sheep farming meant
that wool would be fulled, carded and spun. Adamthwaite Farm (Plate
18) has a workshop and projecting gallery for spinning where the
women could sit while the men were out on the fells.

In poorer or earlier communities, the longhouse would be of a single
storey. The dwellings remaining at the clachan of Auchindrain show
how families lived well into this century. The sleeping room was set
apart with a closet or curtain around the parents' bed. The kitchen, with
its cooking hearth, opened from this room, but only had a simple screen

18. ADAMTHWAITE FARM, Howgill Fells, Sedbergh, Cumbria,
with spinning gallery

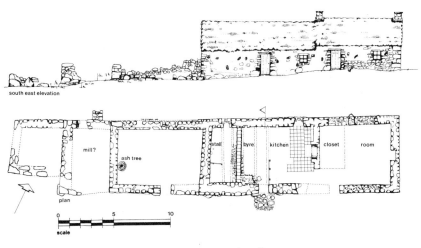

south east elevation

mill?

ash tree

stall   byre   kitchen   closet   room

plan

0   5   10

scale

19. DWELLING AT AUCHINDRAIN CLACHAN, Argyll
(see also Plates 11 and 12)

to separate it from the byre, with its runnel across the floor to the stall.
Adjacent, but ruined, was the barn, a mill and an outbuilding (see Plate
9).

Buildings similar to the stone longhouses were built of brick or of
timber frame in other regions. Farmhouses in the Netherlands, such as
those at Staphorst and at Kadoelen near Zwolk, show typical plan forms

20. PLANS of (a) STAPHORST, and (b) KADOELEN FARMHOUSES, Netherlands
    c. 1800

(Plate 20)—both now re-erected at Arnhem in the Netherlands Open
Air Museum (Het Nederlands Openluchtmuseum, Rijksmuseum voor
Volkskunde)—originally built about 1800 with brick and thatch construction. The dwellings are set apart from the stock and crops, but there
is little to separate the air spaces. Living under one roof allowed for
simplicity of construction, for shared warmth, and for close supervision. The latter is both for stock management and against marauders,
whether man or carnivore. In any case, traditional farming evoked a
close affinity between the family and their stock—something that is
unacceptable to those who live with concepts of modern hygiene. Yet
many of these dwellings are still satisfactory and comfortable.

The Courtyard Farm

Farmsteads, in the Romantic tradition, nestle into the contours of the
landscape. The steading was a refuge. It would be set out to give
protection both from the weather and from marauders. Farming, set
apart from village settlements, could be an isolated life. Self-sufficiency

21. HOF BILSTEIN, Kanton Baselland, Switzerland

was the priority: help in most emergencies was too far away. Survival had to be within the family unit. Thus, farmstead and homestead were synonymous.

Each steading would have a barn for crop storage set high against the prevailing cold winds. The barn would have high cart-doors opening both to the outer and the inner world. Attached to the ends of the barn would be cartsheds, open-sided away from the sun and facing the fields. In some regions, the cartsheds were known as the helme. Wings set out at right angles would provide winter quarters for the livestock. Some of these buildings would open directly into the yard so that cattle, sheep, pigs and poultry could exercise in its sheltered space. The medley of yarded animals and deep litter straw over cobbles has been portrayed by many artists. Low buildings or walls, including the yard gates, would enclose the southern side, permitting the winter sun to penetrate. The trackway from the fields or village would cross the in-bye paddocks and the farmhouse kitchen often looked out over this entrance to the farm. The farmhouse dairy opened into the farmyard.

Something similar to this steading can be found throughout history. It was a well-tried formula. In 1951, a pottery model of such a farmstead

22. **THE TRADITIONAL FARMYARD**, delt. J. T. Sheridan

was found at Cheng-chou in Honan, China, from the Eastern Han Dynasty (first century AD) (Plate 23). The model measures 930×930×760 millimetres. The layout has its granary opposite the farmhouse. There are two dovecotes-cum-watchtowers, a cattle shelter and other buildings enclosing the court for the livestock. The buildings modelled would have been of compressed earth or burnt brick, constructed in a simple trabeated form, and with overlapping and semi-cylindrical tiles. The latter had been invented six centuries earlier. Doves perch on the ridge tiles.

23. FARMSTEAD MODEL, Honan, China
1st century AD

24. GALLY GAP FARM, Malton, North Yorkshire
18th century

A Yorkshire farmstead of some seventeen centuries later is not so different (Plate 24). It is of local stone and pantile. Warring tribes are of the past and the house, still in command of the steading, is set apart. The high barn, with adjoining cartshed and loft, still shelters the court. There are enclosing stock-buildings and stores. A place still exists for the doves. Some later cattle shelters have given extra roofing across the courtyard. Such steadings were typical of the mixed farms following the eighteenth-century enclosures.

Agricultural experts, who advised farmers after the revolution of the field enclosures and new cultivation techniques of the eighteenth century, nearly always recommended the courtyard steading. Arthur Young was no exception. In the ninth volume of his *Annals of Agriculture* of 1799, he illustrated a larger farmstead grouped formally around two courtyards (Plate 25). It included constructional details invented by W. Pitt in 1787. The house is set forward and reflects a simple, country Georgian style. The enclosure of farm buildings measures some 80×30 metres and, to the north, has an extensive ten-bay corn barn and adjoining cart sheds. The fold yards would have been well littered by straw after threshing and the muck would have been carted out at the time of the spring ploughing.

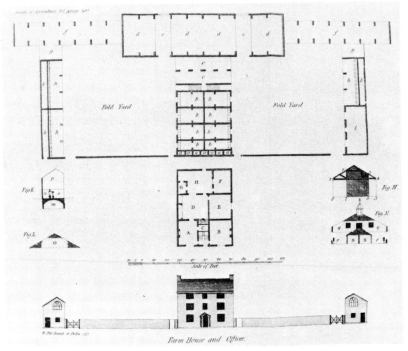

25. IMPROVED FARMSTEAD, Arthur Young, *Annals of Agriculture*, 1799

Model courtyard farmsteads were built throughout the nineteenth century. Childerley Hall (Plate 26) is typical of many estate farms. The Great Hall is of the fifteenth or sixteenth century. Here, Cromwell and Fairfax interrogated Charles I in the Civil War. The main farm buildings have been pulled down and a new range of three stock yards erected. At their centre is a three-storied flour mill with its tall, steam-engine exhaust stack. To the sides of the courts are the beef cattle shelters (and some extra twentieth-century covered space). To the north is the long range of barns with two threshing midstreys. Beyond is the rick yard (see page 70). To the right of the trees, a rick is being built by elevator powered by a horse gin-gang. Adjacent are the treed paddocks and the field trackways to the arable land. On the right, the farm foreman has his house, set to supervise the main entrance to the steading and the valuable vegetable yard and stables. The estate owner is removed from the bustle of activity, with his main windows looking south over lawns and trees, and with his own conservatory for ornamental plants.

Childerley Hall showed the romantic concept of pastoral, estate farming of only one generation ago. The image seemed timeless. Loudon was fascinated by the ordered way of new farm management to be found

26. CHILDERLEY HALL, Cambridgeshire, in 1953

in early nineteenth-century farmsteads. He illustrated many model layouts to suit all styles (see Plate 146). He showed a layout for Northumbrian husbandry which included a farmhouse and farmery suited for fourteen ploughs (Plates 27 and 28). It was designed by Mr. Green, architect. The great estate farms had to have comprehensive facilities for livestock, storage and maintenance of the estate. It was not unusual to include a cartwright and a blacksmith. They had full-time work and the village was too distant. Instant repair was vital—as it is today—during tillage and harvest. The farmer would be an important member of the rural community and his great house would have a position of status. Daily farm management would be the concern of the bailiff—called in Northumberland a 'superintending hind' and in Scotland a 'factor'. But Loudon was not just interested in agriculture. His great Encyclopædia also showed concern for the rural community and illustrated many model farm cottages (Plate 3). He did not like what he saw in Mr. Green's design and, in commenting pungently upon it, cast a shadow of change which later swept the countryside: 'The horses and cows, nay, even the swine, are incomparably better lodged, considering their scale in creation, than the unfortunate occupant of the small cottage here shewn: but the farmers of Northumberland, like those of Scotland, are under the dominion of an all-powerful aristocracy, and their servants are little better than serfs.' He complained that the farmhouse had twenty-eight windows to twenty-eight rooms, but the poor blacksmith had only one window to one room. Concern for the farm-

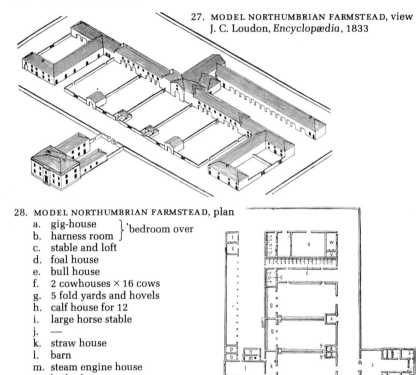

27. MODEL NORTHUMBRIAN FARMSTEAD, view
J. C. Loudon, *Encyclopædia*, 1833

28. MODEL NORTHUMBRIAN FARMSTEAD, plan

a.   gig-house   ⎫ 'bedroom over
b.   harness room ⎭
c.   stable and loft
d.   foal house
e.   bull house
f.   2 cowhouses × 16 cows
g.   5 fold yards and hovels
h.   calf house for 12
i.   large horse stable
j.   —
k.   straw house
l.   barn
m.   steam engine house
n.   boiler house
o.   tool house
p.   poultry house
q.   barn stair
r.   cart shed
s.   cartwright shop
t.   blacksmith
u.   hay yard
v.   bailiff's house
w.   bailiff's cottage
x.   turnip house
y.   pig house
z.   kitchen court and rick yard

worker was not unknown when Victoria came to the throne, but many still were provided with simple shacks or lived in rough hovels or bothies. This apart, the great farm showed a fine command of order and management, each of the fold-yard units holding thirty to fifty cattle of different ages. Whether large or small, the courtyard farm contained the same basic principles of layout. At the grander scale, the court could be entered by great, arched doors as in the eighteenth-century farm in Belgium (Plate 29). Courtyard layouts were created for shelter. They

29. FARMSTEAD, Belgium
    18th century

30. FARMSTEAD, Beauce, France

were sufficient for herded livestock, even with good entrances for the horse and cart. The modern tractor and attachment may be able to use the same access, but the total alteration of the landscape caused by mechanization can be seen around the isolated farmstead in the corn-lands of the Beauce in France (Plate 30).

The basic layout, with too many sharp-cornered entrances and nar-row doorways, typical of the old courtyards, seldom proves satisfactory for the modern, mechanized farm. The courtyard farm has become an anachronism. The great courtyard model farm at Coleshill (Plate 74) is now redundant for farming, being converted to other uses, such as estate workshop and storage for the National Trust, its owners, and light industry, workshops and studios.

Linear Layouts

Processes for the handling of materials are the crux of the modern farm. The basis for these are the tractor and various types of conveyor. Except for liquids, linear planning is best. Even the handling of liquids, such as milk, is best with few bends in the pipes. Bends are harder to keep clean.

31. NORWOOD LODGE FARM, Weeley Heath, Essex
    1974

The aerial view of Norwood Lodge Farm (Plate 31) demonstrates how
modern buildings tend to be in rectangular blocks around an access
road. The semblance of a court arrangement near the farmhouse
remains. Nearby are signs of post-war development with narrow, steel-
trussed buildings. Two sets of wide-span portal-framed buildings are
opposite, probably from the 1950s. Produce is palletted and pallets are
stacked alongside the buildings as temporary storage. In the 1960s, a
large grain unit seems to have been established with a nest of bins plus a
large elevator house, probably with milling equipment. Some expansion seems to have taken place. There is a larger silo, attached by
conveyor but set apart. A bund holds water. Since this seems to be an
all-arable farm, it is unlikely to be effluent and irrigation would be
desirable. Nearby are two Nissen huts, which presumably provided
cheap overflow potato-storage in the early 1970s. Though this analysis
is by deduction, the overall linearity of layout is obvious.

A different type of linear layout is shown in the dairy unit for 600

32. DAIRY UNIT, Nettlebed, Oxfordshire   1974

cows established by the late Peter Fleming at Nettlebed in the 1960s
(Plate 32). Essential for management is the handling of cows in batches
according to their capacity for milk yield. Thus, rows of identical
kennels house the batches, from which the cows enter open yards
containing rows of mangers for feeding. A kennel is a cheap structure
where cubicle divisions support a monopitch roof. The mangers are
filled by self-unloading trailers which back alongside them. The taller
building is the collecting yard and milking parlours, through which the
cows pass twice a day before returning to their yards. Such large
numbers of cows cannot be allowed to graze, since they would have to
disperse too far from the fixed equipment for milking. They are housed
almost permanently within the layout, grass being 'zero-grazed' and
brought to them daily in the summer, with roots, silage or hay in the
winter.

The concept of mass production within a linear layout was taken to
extremes in the great feedlots of mid-west America. In units such as at
Monfort, 100,000 head of steers were fattened during the 1960s (Plates
33 and 34). More recently, such units have become to some extent
uneconomic, due to the cost of concentrate feeds. The case of the
Arizona and Colorado Land and Cattle Company illustrates how such
feedlots worked. It started on 100 hectares adjacent to a railway in
Queen Creek in 1966 (Plates 35 and 36). It held 60,000 head, selling off
330 each day. These required 20,000 tonnes of grain and 5000 tonnes of
hay every month. The former was delivered daily in seven rail trucks.
The mill-mix plant operated around the clock. Thirty men worked in

33. FEEDLOT, Monfort, USA, in the foreground reinforced-concrete
tower silo of 1920, unused   1970

34. FEEDLOT, Monfort, close-up of pens

35. QUEEN CREEK, Phoenix, Arizona, USA
1973

36. DRIED GRASS CUBES for Queen Creek feedlot

shifts to produce 1000 tonnes of meal each day, some of which was for sale. Each pen, or corral, measured 55×45 metres or 55×68 metres, to hold 250–300 head, depending on age. These were laid out in seventeen blocks, divided by trailer alleys. In addition to the meal, 30,000 tonnes of dried grass cubes were fed each year, being stacked in 2500-tonne heaps every 100 metres around the perimeter.

The normal European cattle-building for about a hundred head, seems a modest enterprise. But cattle feeding with a self-unloading trailer, filled from the chute from a tower silo (Plates 37 and 38) and

37. CATTLE UNIT, Sweffling, Suffolk
1967

38. TOP UNLOADER to concrete stave tower silo. A Reco-Clay unloader, with a
three-point suspension, and with double auger (cover removed) within a
6-metre diameter tower, sweeping silage to the outlet hopper into the chute
on the outside.

39.
SELF-UNLOADING
TRAILER,
Sweffling, Suffolk
1967

40.
JOG-THROUGH
FEEDER
1967

41.
AUGER FEEDER
1964

delivering silage into mangers down the centre of a building, does need linear planning. Mechanized cattle-feeding has three main systems, each of which works best with uninterrupted runs of manger of up to about 100 metres in length (Plate 39 to 41).

A simplified layout for a farm of about 400 hectares and based mainly on corn, milk and baconers is shown in Plate 42. A farm of this size might support several enterprises. It might need, for example, storage for 700 tonnes of grain, housing for 240 cows plus about 180 followers to the herd (calves and heifers), housing for a breeding herd of 120 sows, with their progeny of 1500 baconers, together with a potato store for 1000 tonnes, and full supporting services. What the layout demonstrates is that there needs to be a main spine road linking the highway to the fields. Around this can be grouped a wide range of disparate and separate buildings. Many of these are rectangular and require access right through them as well as around them. Trailers, even tractors, require large turning circles so that buildings need to be set apart. This may also be essential both for hygiene and as a fire precaution. It should be clear that there can be no similarity between such a modern farm layout and the historic courtyard. Conversion, alteration and extension of the latter, to meet the requirements of modern mechanization, let alone size of unit, inevitably means that the buildings will lose both coherence and beauty. This is one reason why modern improvements within a farmstead tend to look disruptive. Linear layouts do destroy the homogeneity of the courtyard.

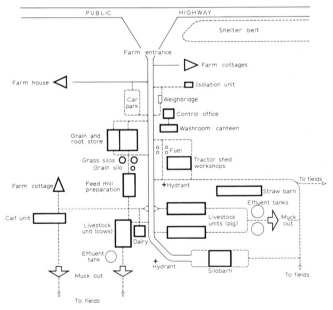

42. DIAGRAM PLAN FOR LARGE MIXED FARM

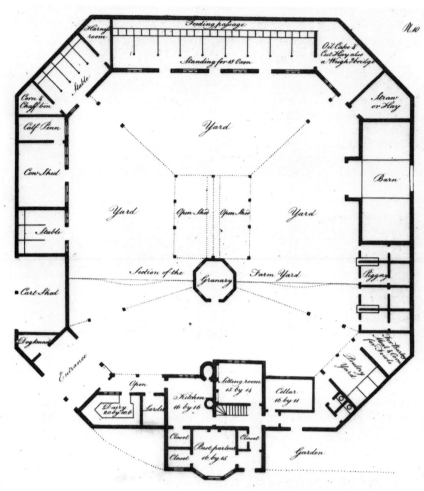

43. LUGAR'S OCTAGONAL FARMSTEAD
1807

Radial Layouts

The potential of organizing work within a radial layout, whether circular or polygonal, and whether in the field or a building, has attracted
many farmers. An ambitious, circular stack-yard was shewn by Arthur
Young in 1799 (see Plates 93 and 94). Richard Lugar illustrated an
octagonal piggery around a steam cooker in 1807 (see Plate 144). In his
same *Country Gentleman's Architect*, he went further in showing an
octagonal farmstead with a central barn and granary and three fold-
yards and a general yard (Plate 43). A continuous range of buildings for

44. SHAKER BARN, Hancock, USA
 1824

all the stock and storage, including the farmhouse, with its observation windows into the yards, was to be set around the perimeter. Not everyone appreciated such flights of imagination, though several geometrically planned farm buildings were erected. C. Hassall was the Board of Agriculture surveyor for Monmouth and, in his *General View of the Agriculture* for that county in 1812 he wrote that buildings 'fantastically planned in sweeps, semi-circles, octagons and pentagons ... look pretty on paper but when you come to construct them a good deal of difficulty occurs in roofing and a great deal of room is thrown away which cannot be applied to any beneficial purpose'.

This practical viewpoint was not accepted in North America where a number of great, circular barns are a distinctive building type. Most are of the nineteenth century, particularly from the second half of that century, and many were built by the Shakers. Eric Sloane, in his *An Age of Barns* suggested that 'the Shakers used the circle in their inspirational drawings.... they took a delight in round hats, rugs and boxes. ... there is a saying that the round barn was intended to keep the devil from hiding in corners.' Whatever the reason, some of the round barns are dramatic buildings. A few are built around a central silo, others have a central barn as in the Shaker barn at Hancock, Massachussetts (Plate 44). This was probably the first such barn, built in 1824 and rebuilt in 1865. Eight great posts, with four trusses, support the clerestory lantern. An inner ring of posts reduces the clear diameter by some 7 metres, to leave a clear central mow of over 14.5×9 metres in height to where the rafters radiate. At about the same period, J. Lockhart Morton illustrated several circular plantations and buildings in his *A Series of Designs for*

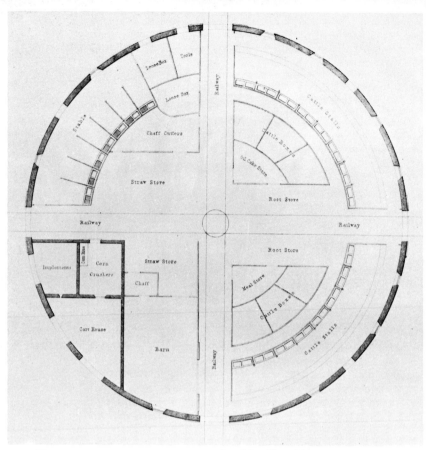

Labels within the plan (clockwise from top): Loose Box, Tools, Loose Box, Chaff Cutters, Stable, Straw Store, Cattle Stelle, Cattle Boxes, Oil Cake Store, Root Store, Railway, Railway, Railway, Root Store, Cattle Boxes, Meal Store, Cattle Stelle, Railway, Implements, Corn Crushers, Corn Store, Straw Store, Chaff, Cart House, Barn

45. CIRCULAR COVERED HOMESTALL, plan, J. Lockhart Morton

Farm Buildings and Plantations (c. 1820–30), including a suitable scheme for a 250-acre farm (Plate 45).

Circular dovecotes (Plate 46) go back through medieval times into antiquity. They are a specialized type of intensive livestock building, the forerunner to modern factory production. Doves and pigeons provided eggs and meat, especially through the winter. Cotes were introduced into England by the Normans and, by the seventeenth century, there were some 26,000. Many were elaborate structures, lined internally with ledges or holes set within the walling for over 1000 birds in larger cotes. Access to the eggs was from a ladder rotated from a central shaft known as a potence. Hence a circular building was desirable though other shapes were known in some parts of the world (see Plate 221). The doves are accessible from the roof lantern. By the eighteenth century, root crops were beginning to make cotes less essential since other forms of winter meat became available.

Henry Stephens in his Book of the Farm, published in 1871, sketched a circular stell set around a haystack and with a 2-metre high perimeter

46. DOVECOTE, Avebury, Wiltshire (see also Plate 221)
c. 17th century

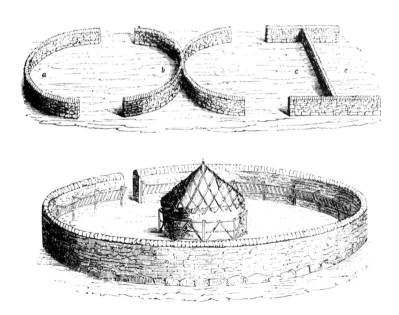

47. SHEEP STELL, Henry Stephens, *Book of the Farm*, 1871

48. SHEEP STELL
1971

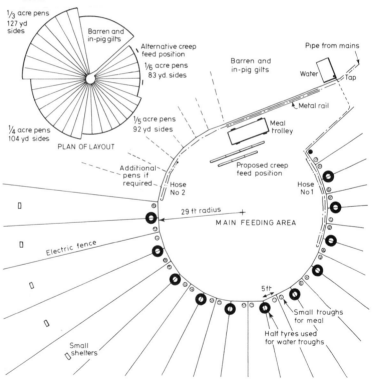

¹/₃ acre pens
127 yd
sides

Barren and
in-pig gilts

Alternative creep
feed position

¹/₆ acre pens
83 yd. sides

Barren and
in-pig gilts

Pipe from mains

Water

Tap

Metal rail

¹/₅ acre pens
92 yd sides

Meal
trolley

PLAN OF LAYOUT

¹/₄ acre pens
104 yd sides

Additional
pens if
required

Proposed creep
feed position

Hose
No 2

Hose
No 1

29 ft radius

MAIN FEEDING AREA

Electric fence

5 ft

Small troughs
for meal

Half tyres used
for water troughs

Small
shelters

49. RADIAL LAYOUT FOR PIG ARKS
1958

50. SHEEP RACE, New Zealand
    1980

wall of stone, topped by turves with its own capping stone. Hayracks
lined the wall internally, except for the small gateway. At the centre was
the haystack. Such Highland stells, if some 18 metres in diameter, could
hold ten score of sheep or, overnight, up to sixteen score. Today, stells
are prefabricated in metal.

Imperial Chemical Industries made a work-study investigation of Mr.
Peter Smith's Staffordshire pig farm in 1958. This showed that a radial
layout of moveable arks divided by electric fences which could be
moved fron site to site on a rotational grassland policy, was more
efficient than rectangular, traditional paddocks. With a circular work
area of 20 metres diameter for a feed trailer and some thirty paddocks,
each with its ark for a sow, the distance walked by the pigman for
feeding was reduced to 25 per cent for the same number of sows (Plate
49). Sheep handling of large flocks requires careful penning for dipping
and other treatment. Mr. John Gallagher's layout is for 4000 sheep
designed so that he can work alone (Plate 50). There are three sets of
yards, each 63×40 metres, with one end set as a semi-circle to form a
race to the drenching tank.

Storage bins for grain, with modern auger elevators, make a radial
layout sensible. Full or part circles of bins have been seen on many
farms since the 1950s.

Circular or rotary milking parlours were introduced in the late 1960s.
Cows moved round on a platform from the cowman's work position.
Each rotation was planned to allow a cow to give all her milk, usually in

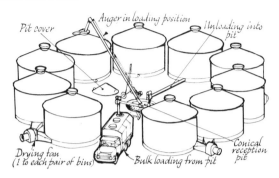

51. RADIAL GRAIN BINS, diagrammatic sketch.

52. VIEW OF RADIAL BINS being filled, 1966. Power Farming

53. CIRCULAR COLLECTING YARD AND MILKING PARLOURS, Fontanarosa. 1972

54. RUTGERS UNIVERSITY COW UNIT, New Brunswick, USA
   1972

a period of seven or eight minutes. Most milking parlours of this kind are put into normal buildings. One circular building was formed out of standard metal plates normally used for slurry tanks (see Plate 179). The collecting yard where cows are held prior to being milked is often circular, with a rotating gate from the centre pushing the herd towards the parlour entrance.

Experiments in circular forms and construction have continued for several types of building. The great revolving drum in a circular glass tower is one experiment (see Plate 72). An experimental circular dairy unit for up to forty cows, with a diameter of about 19 metres, complete with a central tower silo nearly 19 metres tall and set above a 3-metre high self-feeding manger, was built in the early 1970s (Plate 54). Perimeter posts to hold the cranked roof are set at 10° intervals. Between tower and outer wall are feeding area, slatted exercise and circulation area, and cubicles for the cows. It was designed by research engineers at Rutgers University with insulated roofs of coated urethane over honeycomb panels and with insulated plywood wall panels.

The Rick Yard

From the time of the Napoleonic Wars, the rick-yard controversy began to be debated. The idea of keeping unthreshed corn in sheaves goes back to biblical times. Barns to hold the sheaves were built by the Romans. But the idea of stacking the sheaves in the open, in rectangular or round mounds, then of thatching the tops like a cottage to keep out the wet, must have evolved in the medieval period. Placing the stacks to assist threshing by wind power was considered in the late eighteenth century (see Plate 93). But the idea of the rick yard as an adjunct to the farmstead, eventually making the large barn redundant, evolved in the early nineteenth century. It was reported in 1804 as a matter for debate by Dr. Hunter whose opinions were discussed four decades later by the Revd. J. M. Wilson in his own *Rural Cyclopedia* of 1847 in which he described the virtues of rick yard over barn:

> The barns of Great Britain were formerly of so large a capacity as to contain all the produce of farms, whether grain or fodder; and even so late as about 30 or 40 years ago, such enormous barns were regarded by many farmers as essential to their prosperity. Dr Hunter, who published six volumes of Geographical Essays in 1804, occupies an entire essay with the refutation of the reasons which were usually urged by these farmers—that corn can be built at less expense in the house than in the rickyard, that it is better protected in the former than the latter, and that the storing of it in the house is much more convenient for threshing. But modern improvements in rick building, in thrashing, and in the arrangement of farmeries, have convinced the most hesitating, that the rickyard is both the cheaper and the better place for the great bulk of the produce, and that the barn is needed only for the operations of threshing.... Some barns, even in excellent farming districts, have a width of only 18 ft within the walls, but no really good barn has a width of less than 20 feet.

The great rick yards became a familiar sight in arable districts. That at Childerley Hall was typical of High Victorian corn management (see Plate 26). Though such layouts, usually north from the old steadings, continued well into the 1950s they have now disappeared from farm practice. The rick yard was a large area, normally screened round by trees, of well-drained rubble laid to a low camber to drain off to an edge ditch. The rubble was grassed over except for the main trackway from the fields down to the barn. In many counties, the elm used to provide the tree screen and this grouping of protective elms became a distinct marker for the steading in the landscape.

There was always a difference between corn used for man and that fed to livestock. This distinction was reflected in the layout of buildings. With the discovery that straw could be threshed by machine came the realization that rolled corn was more economical as feed. In turn, this made the rick yard more popular. This important change of attitude was finely observed by H. S. Thompson of the Moat Hall, near Borough-

55. RICK ON STADDLE STONES AND PLATFORM, Brandon, Hampshire

bridge, Yorkshire, who was both a judge and a life governor of the Royal Agricultural Society of England. He wrote in the *Journal* an essay on farm buildings in 1850:

> All the plans now published the old method of building round a rectangular area, and using the enclosure as a straw-yard, has been given up or very much modified. The cause of this change is obvious: so long as farm horses were fed on unground corn and uncut hay or straw, it was only necessary that the stable should be conveniently placed with respect to the barn and the haystack; and when cattle were wintered chiefly on straw, which was supplied to them direct from the barn door, the old fashioned square yard, surrounded by buildings, was probably the best that could have been adopted. . . .
>
> By degrees, however, it was discovered that if the horse corn were ground and the fodder cut into chaff, not only was the food consumed with less waste . . . and the animal power economised . . . it may be stated generally that it is found profitable to call in the aid of machinery and to make the business of a farm approximate more closely to that of a manufactory. The necessary consequence of this change of system is a great increase of intercommunication between the different buildings of a farm.

There were two main threats to the rick yard—fire and rats. Heaps of damp straw, subjected to hot sun, could combust, and fire was the dread of any farmer. Damp hay was at even greater risk of spontaneous combustion. Stacks of inflammable material have always been a magnet for arsonists and small boys playing with matches. It was an easy place to harm your enemy. John Masefield summed up the spirit of vengeance in one of his pastoral poems:

> I will bloody him, I will bloody fix
> I will bloody burn his bloody ricks.

56. STONE PLATFORM FOR RICK

No threat could be more dire or cut to a farmer's wellbeing more sharply. Rick yards were sited to be away from the prevailing wind's path to the steading. Rats were another problem. The idea of placing the rick above the ground on anti-rat supports with flared tops has uncertain origins. The staddle stones of the Cotswolds and West Country became a feature of the steadings. Their mushroom shape and timber platform kept the rats out of the corn. Alternatively, solid platforms could be built with an overhanging lip (Plate 56). This was quite common in Wales. Prefabricated platforms of malleable iron set on cast-iron pillars were the answer for districts without suitable stone. Thomas Pearson & Co. introduced their patent rick devices in 1863 and it was possible to purchase rectangular or circular frames of any size. Corrugated-iron rick covers instead of thatch saved time, though denied a country craft. As Thomas Pearson advertised, these roofs doubled up as temporary stock-pen roofing at other times of the year. As one customer testified, having placed his rick near a railway, it was showered by sparks from a passing train, but it was saved from disaster by having a fireproof cover instead of thatch.

The layout of the stack yard to provide maximum efficiency was a matter of concern to the great Victorian farm improvers. Sir Thomas Tancred Bt. received a Royal Agricultural Society prize for his essay on

THOMAS PEARSON & CO.'S HARVESTING APPLIANCES.

Patent
Corrugated
and
Galvanized
Iron Rick
Covers—
Thatch Dis-
pensing,
Rain Proof,
Fire Proof,
and
Removeable

These
Covers are
simple in
construction
easily
handled.
A Rick of
say 60 feet
by 15 feet
is
covered in
the matter
of a few
hours.

No pillars or supports are necessary, as they rest simply on the rick, and are tightly bound down by means of pins and chains. Since T. P. & Co. introduced their invention in 1863, large numbers of these Covers have been sold to the Members of the Royal Agricultural Society from whom the most encouraging and perhaps too flattering testimony has been received to their *practicability* and *utility*. In illustration of this, one gentleman, Mansfeldt De C. Elmshall, Esq., of Pwl Piran, states that the Iron Cover served a *twofold* purpose, namely, after doing duty as a covering for his rick, it made a capital roof for a cattle-shed ; and John Harward, Esq., of Kidderminster, writes that he found it *eminently serviceable* ; first as a cover for his stack, and afterwards as a roof for a moveable sheep-pen, in which, to quote his own words, " his early ewes and lambs were comfortably housed throughout the winter." While another customer characterizes them as *invaluable* where the stackyard is in the vicinity of a railway, and assures T. P. & Co. that his stackyard, buildings, &c., might have been destroyed but for the circumstance that he had one of these Rick Covers in use (120 feet long) at a perilous moment, when a disastrous fire seemed unavoidable—a shower of sparks from the engine of a passing train were carried by the wind in the direction of the Rick Yard and blown on top of the iron cover, which, being thoroughly fireproof, prevented any damage being done, and thus *the whole property may be said to have been saved by means of this simple appliance.*

Patent
oblong Corn
Rick Stands
with
Malleable

Iron Frames
and Cast
Iron Pillars,
about 7d.
per square
foot.

Made any length or breadth. No stackyard should be without these stands ; they form the best *invest-ment* the farmer can make, as they pay themselves in a year or two, especially where the steading is over-run with rats and mice. They enable the Corn to be stacked sooner in wet weather.

Circular
Corn Rick
Stands run
about
the
same price

as the
Oblongs.
Pillars for
Wood Frames
3s. to 4s.
each.

Intending Purchasers, by ordering now, can have them delivered by June, or earlier, in time to have them properly fitted up and ready for Harvest.

Detailed Prices from T. PEARSON & Co., 71, Queen Street, Glasgow.

C

57. PEARSON'S PATENT HARVESTING APPLIANCES
1863

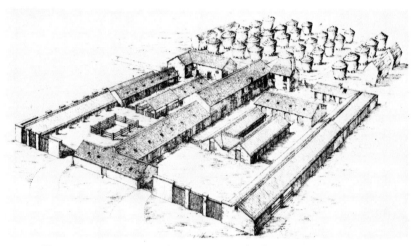

58. SIR THOMAS TANCRED'S MODEL FARM, bird's-eye view
1850

the 'Construction of Farm Buildings' which was published in the *Journal* in 1850. He described and illustrated his own model farm (Plates 58 and 59): 'The stack yard thus contained the raw material out of which the chief products of the farm (viz. the grain, the fat meat, and the manure) are to be obtained, we convey the sheaves on a truck along the rails to the elevator, which raises them to the threshing machine, the grain being delivered below into sacks ready dressed for market, and the straw carried forwards on the upper storey into the straw barn ... on the left hand on entering is the power employed on the farm, viz. the engine and horses ... in the central parts and to the right hand are the grain, the fatting beasts, the dairy—beyond are the open sheds and yards.' The stack yard had rectangular ricks for sheep, horses and cows and round corn stacks of 12-foot diameter. All were on staddle stones and the thirty corn stacks were set in rows to the sides of tram and cart tracks. The sheaves were forked on to trucks. The layouts of all the buildings were placed with equal care to reduce labour and to assist mechanization. The buildings were designed by H. S. Thompson, who also had much to say about rick yards, as quoted above.

A. B. Denton illustrated in detail how to mechanize the rick yard in his book *The Farm Homesteads of England* which he published in 1863 (Plate 60). All the ricks were built above trackways. This was an improvement on Tancred's layout where stacks had to be dismantled and double handled. Denton's tramways could be set below ground or be linked above ground by curves or by a turntable. All the stacks were moved bodily into the great, arched stack shed for steam threshing. The

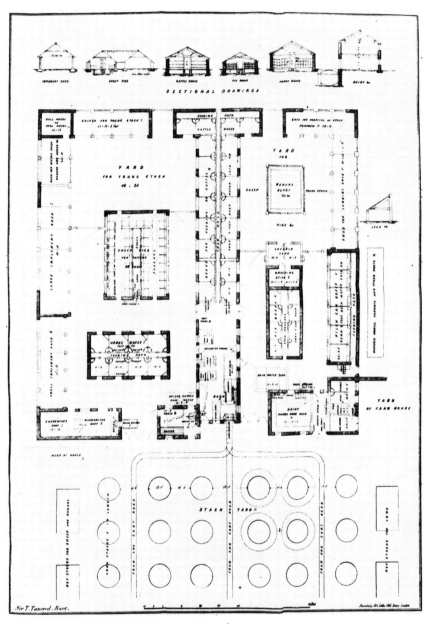

59. SIR THOMAS TANCRED'S MODEL FARM, plan

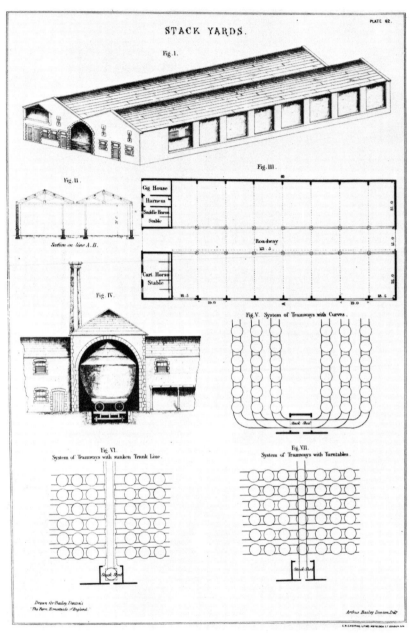

60. **TRACKED RICK YARDS**, A. B. Denton, *The Farm Homesteads of England*,
1863

61. GROUP OF DUTCH BARNS

62. DEMONSTRATION BARN, Arnhem Museum

BY HER MAJESTY'S ROYAL LETTERS PATENT.

F. M^cNEILL AND CO.,

ONLY PATENTEES AND MANUFACTURERS OF

IMPROVED PATENT ASPHALTED FELT.

(FACTORY, LAMB'S BUILDINGS, BUNHILL ROW, LONDON.)

The MANUFACTURERS beg to call the attention of Landed Proprietors, Farmers, Graziers, Nurserymen, Architects, Builders, Emigrants, and the Public generally, to their

IMPROVED PATENT ASPHALTED FELT

FOR ROOFING

Houses, Cottages, Verandas, Out-Buildings, Sheds,

AND EVERY OTHER DESCRIPTION OF BUILDING,

IN LIEU OF SLATES, TILES, THATCH, ZINC, ETC.

The FELT is also in great demand, and highly approved of, for lining Granaries and Storehouses, for covering Garden Sheds and Frames, and Corn and Hay Ricks. It is also a protection to Ceilings under Flooring from Wet and Damp, at the same time Deadening Sound; and is particularly adapted for Exportation to the Colonies, where it is now extensively used; and when used under Slates or Tiles, adds greatly to the warmth and durability of the Building.

The great superiority of this article over every other description of Roofing, consists in its CHEAPNESS, LIGHTNESS, ELASTICITY, WARMTH, and DURABILITY. It has been exhibited at the great Agricultural Shows of England, Scotland, and Ireland, and obtained the prize for being the best article for Roofing, to supersede Slates, Tiles, Thatches, &c. &c.

Samples, with full directions as to its uses, and the manner of applying it, with Testimonials from, and reference to, Gentlemen who have extensively used it, sent free to any part of the Town or Country.

*** The price of the Roofing Felt is only One Penny per Square Foot, which is considerably less than half the expense of Tiles and Slates; besides which, there is an immense saving effected in the expense of carriage and laying on, and particularly in the Timber necessary to support the Roof, as the weight of the Felt is only about 25lbs. to the 100 square feet.

This Felt is composed of the strongest and most durable materials, and is saturated with the BEST OF ASPHALTE OR BITUMEN (THE SAME AS SELECTED AND USED BY SIR ISAMBERT BRUNEL FOR THE THAMES TUNNEL, BEING FOUND THE MOST ELASTIC AND EFFECTIVE RESISTER OF WET).

PATENT FELT MANUFACTORY,
Lamb's Buildings, Bunhill Row, London, March, 1844.

[*Jan.* 1845]   *D*

63. M'NEILL'S PATENT ROOFING
1844

total number of tracked systems installed is not known but it is believed that none survive.

Denton also observed, in his description of homesteads, how the Dutch barn was 'deservedly growing in favour, though at a slow rate'. The prefabricated steel barn, with its light, curved roof of corrugated iron, became the mainstay of farm storage during the 1880s. It has become a traditional feature of the countryside because of its relative cheapness and adaptability. But the idea of having a 'roof on stilts' to cover hay, sometimes corn, has evolved over 400 years. It does seem to be a Dutch characteristic for, as Sir Hugh Platt described in the late sixteenth century, for generations they had used a barn with a roof 'hanging upon postes ... with pinnes and winches' so that it could be kept immediately over the top of the stack. Such barns feature in seventeenth-century Dutch paintings and are a common feature today.

Sir Hugh Platt built a similar barn on his Hertfordshire farm and a number of others have been built in England. They were featured in 1844 in an advertisement in the *Royal Agricultural Advertiser*. The firm of F. M'Neill & Co. had patented asphalted felt and they 'beg to call the attention of Landed Proprietors, Farmers, Graziers, Nurserymen, Architects, Builders, Emigrants, and the Public generally' to such a cheap and durable roofing material which could cost only one penny per square foot (Plate 63).

2 Primary and Secondary Power Sources

In all histories of technology, the Industrial Revolution is seen as a watershed. Most historians consider the period from the invention of the wheel in prehistory up to the harnessing of coal to smelt iron to be one epoch, though this is not so in terms of politics, exploration or even science. For technology, the period from 1775 to 1975 may be seen as a second epoch, and the evolution of the computer to become a commonplace tool during the 1970s must mark another watershed equal in its impact on society to the invention of the wheel and of cast iron.

In agriculture, the wheel certainly provoked a fundamental change. The introduction of the plough was probably of equal importance and Jethro Tull's seed-drill of 1701 marked another vital change in agricultural practice. But the Industrial Revolution was more dramatic in relation to agricultural technology. It introduced new sources of power into the fields and steadings, and, moreover, the mass distribution of equipment from factories standardized rural techniques over large areas.

Primitive agriculture throughout the world depends on natural or muscular sources of power. Natural energy, when harnessed from the sun, gravity, water or wind, is considered to be from primary sources. When set in motion it needs no further secondary effort. The latter comes when muscle is applied to the task, either by man himself or by the beasts he has trained for the purpose. The beasts normally used are oxen, donkeys and horses, though in certain places others, like elephants, may be trained for specific tasks.

The development of technology, in one sense, has been to increase output. In another, its chief benefit is to reduce manual labour. Ideally, it does both. The period before fossil fuels, before steam, may be considered primitive since output was limited to the capacity of the primary and secondary power sources. Though the image of farmwork is surrounded by a mist of romantic toil, the reality was otherwise. Natural power had limitations and, as any miller would have testified, included its own back-breaking associated work. Muscle power of man and beast, in many cases applied from dawn to dusk with few rest periods, was exerted in all weathers. Survival was a hard task-master.

This part of the book deals with the main sources of power before the Industrial Revolution. Of course, the latter did not totally supplant them. But the history of the last 200 years has turned farming into a work-bench operation—if a tractor seat can be equated thus. Our image is changing. We have coined two new phrases, intermediate and alternative technology, to meet changing circumstances in the last part of this century. Both have their main impetus in assisting the third world countries to support themselves. But, as the crisis over the supply of fossil fuels deepens, their significance for the developed countries sharpens.

Intermediate technology is not based on a rejection of modern, high technology systems. However, it does assert that the latter should not have universal application. Most power should stem from the resources available within an area, using improved forms of simple equipment which can be made locally, without rejecting the use of manual labour. Only a few specialist pieces of equipment, which provide a vital contribution to improved output in association with locally made tools, should be imported from developed countries. In agriculture, the aim is not to have all tillage by tractor but to ensure that man and beast use tools which turn soil with the minimum of friction and therefore of effort. Simple electrical generators may be used but this does not imply the need for a national supply grid for electricity.

Alternative technology accepts more fundamental principles. Essentially, it rejects all fossil fuels and would revert industrial and agricultural production to the use of natural and muscle sources of power. With modern knowledge of physics and of materials, this does not mean a return to output levels available pre-1775.

In 1980, viewpoints about energy—about power—remain confused. Energy based on fossil fuels can never be cheap again. New sources of power could change our philosophy: some are at the edge of science fiction. Equally, old techniques may have new methods. Passive and natural energy are no longer concepts with limited possibilities. Technology is likely to be polarized. High technology will be concentrated where yields will cover its high cost. This has important implications for landscapes and farmsteads. Alternative technologies will coexist, but mainly within poorer terrain. The cost of energy will diminish the mixed, middle-sized farm so common today.

The 1980s will provide a sharp contrast in technological development. High technology, nuclear or otherwise, will continue. The micro-processor rather than the brain will handle data. But solar, wind, water and other natural sources for power will also make a dramatic contribution to our needs. By 1990 it is certain that this book will need to be extended, since the farmstead will be very different from today. Solar and wind power, together with an intermediate technology, will have become the norm on many farms—which may be neighbours to those farms where all work is automated and where fields are operated by robot machines.

PRIMARY (NATURAL) POWER SOURCES

Sun Power

Many advertisements for food draw on the image of goodness in 'sun-kissed' produce. Farmers, though usually unaware of it, are photosynthetic engineers. They show their skill by harnessing the power of the sun, through plants, so as to provide us with carbohydrates and proteins. They also draw trace elements and nutrients out of the soil's chemistry, but, essentially, their science is to capture the sun. Unfortunately, most of the sun's beneficial power goes to waste. It falls either on barren ground or on plants alien to our diet.

In a world stricken by hunger, our aim should be to make photosynthesis through plants increase the energy available from food. But there are problems. In the United Kingdom, for example, our crops absorb only one per cent of the total incidence of solar radiation. And under one-fifth of this is then recovered in the harvested crop. Indeed, the energy obtained from cereals in England—or for that matter from rice in Egypt—is only about one-sixth of that originally absorbed by the crop. Root crops, such as potatoes, are slightly more efficient.

Table I: **Energetics of British Agriculture**

	Mega Joules per annum
Total incidence of solar radiation	$610,000 \times 10^9$
Amount absorbed by whole plants	6100×10^9
Amount recovered in harvested crop	1116×10^9

Based on K. L. Blaxter, *Biologist*, Vol. 22(1), 14, 1975; and J. Heslop-Harrison, *Biologist*, Vol. 22(1), 60, 1975.

Much of this meagre supply of energy is then wasted by man. Nearly one half of the potential value of the harvested crop is lost before it reaches our plate. Such is the penalty of living with convenience foods: better by far is farming self-sufficiency. But, keeping livestock makes matters worse. Feeding cereals to pigs to provide bacon for breakfast, rather than living on porridge, means we receive only 0.03 per cent of the original intake of energy of the corn crop. Even milk only provides 0.05 per cent of the energy falling on the sward of grass. The more civilized and affluent we become, the more we throw away the sun.

Throughout history, farmers have been aware that the sun, provided there is also water, will increase yields. They know that genetics and husbandry are important: but, above all else, the microclimate around

64. LANZAROTE VINEYARD, Canary Islands

the crop will be the key to success. This is why, in northern, temperate
lands, the south-sloping fertile field is the greatest asset. In medieval
England, within the three-field rotation of the feudal village, great care
was taken that each person held equal shares of land sloping to the
south. Similarly, land sub-divided between a man's sons would be split
so that each received part of the most prized cultivation. Thus, fields
were fragmented into less efficient allotments.

In contrast to the land practice of English villeins, there are throughout the world examples of landscapes which have been manipulated so
that the sun could increase yields. For the most part, such manipulation
was hardly architecture. Contour terraces, irrigation dykes, or the
ridge-and-furrow did not require building skills. But the borderline
between topographical change and building can be imprecise. Perhaps
there is no more dramatic example of low profiled 'buildings' than the
vine cultivations on the volcanic island of Lanzarote—that northern-
most outpost of the Canary Islands (Plate 64). Lanzarote is inhospitable.
It is seared by the trade winds that blow regularly at 40 miles an hour,
removing moisture from the arid ground. Much of the island erupted in
1730 and its soil, lacking humus, is rich in mineral ash, but it is difficult
to cultivate. The islanders learnt to spread picon, that is lava gravel, to a
depth of 100–300 millimetres. The shallower depth suits salads, the
latter vines. The gravel was scooped out to form depressions and low

walls of lava stone were built to protect each from the Atlantic winds. Each plant has its own crater, placed to reduce the sun's angle of incidence by day and to collect the precipitation of the wind's humidity by night. Cultivation thus creates a strange architecture for a lunar-like landscape.

Silica, transformed as glass, is the secret by which the power of the sun can be enhanced. The Romans knew this secret. Tiberius, according to Pliny, forced his cucumbers with stoves. These were pits covered with slabs of transparent material. Lucius Columella, too, in his *De Re Rustica* of the mid-first century AD recommended glass for early cucumbers, and Marcus Martialis later, in his studies of the 'sweet life', wrote about the practice of grape houses to force the plants in winter. The practice was not altogether lost in medieval times in France, and it was recorded in a letter signed 'John' that flowers at Bois-le-Duc were grown in glass pavilions which faced the south. This may well be the first definite reference to a greenhouse. Greenhouses came into their own with the development of the orangery, which seems to have been a by-product of the Renaissance. Oranges were known to be of great value for sound health. We know, now, about the value of vitamin C. The earliest orangeries had little glass, relying rather on internal stoves and window shutters. There was a magnificent example at Heidelberg in the seventeenth century, belonging to Solomon de Gaus, and holding 400 orange trees. It measured some 10×125 metres, but it did not, however, concentrate the power of the sun. John Evelyn wrote of greenhouses in 1664 as being suitable for tender flowers or plants. Later that century, in 1696, Thomas Langford published his study *On Fruit Trees* and reported the important transition to a new industry: 'Greenhouses are of late built as Ornaments to Gardens (as Summer and Banqueting houses were formerly) as well as for Conservatories for tender Plants.' The great houses began to have orangeries. Queen Anne had one erected by Vanbrugh in 1704 at Hampton Court. A forcing house with a glass roof had been built by the Duke of Rutland at Belvoir Castle a decade later. At this time most had tall windows and tiled roofs, and in 1731 Phillip Miller published his *Gardener's Dictionary* showing a greenhouse, flanked by two stove rooms, with a tiled roof. A major revision of his work in 1768 replaced the illustration to show a glass-roofed greenhouse.

The breakthrough in the design of greenhouses—if that is not an unfortunate phrase—came with prefabricated, cast-iron construction. John Claudius Loudon was a remarkable man. His famous encyclopaedia on rural architecture of 1833 had a profound effect on farm building design (page 24), but he made his name, both as an inventor and horticulturist, with an earlier work in 1822, *An Encyclopædia of Gardening*. This gave details of the wrought-iron sash-bar he had invented and presented to the Horticultural Society in 1816. This was a year after he had been inspired by Sir George Mackenzie's paper 'On the Form which the Glass of a Forcing-house ought to have in order to receive the greatest possible quantity of Rays from the Sun' in which he stressed: '...make the surface of your green-house roof parallel to the vaulted surface of the heavens, or to the plane of the sun's orbit.' This was a revolutionary idea which challenged Loudon's technical curiosity to master the potential of the sash-bar. He followed this with a number of studies over the next few years:

1817   *Remarks on the Construction of Hothouses*
1818   *A Comparative View of the Common and Curvilinear Modes of Roofing Hothouses*
1819   *Sketches of Curvilinear Hothouses, with a description of the various Purposes in Horticultural and General Architecture, to which a Solid Iron Sash Bar (lately invented) is Applicable*
1824   *The Green-House Companion.*

Loudon built his own home in 1824, a semi-detached villa, Nos. 3 and 5 in Porchester Terrace, Bayswater. This included an ambitious, experimental glasshouse and conservatory (Plate 65) which confirmed his

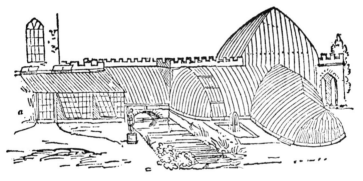

65. PORCHESTER TERRACE VILLA, Bayswater, London
1824

belief, expounded in his *Encyclopaedia of Gardening*, that 'the object of such a junction of different curvatures ... is to show that, in regard to form, the strength and tenacity of the iron bar, and the proper choice of shape in the panes of glass, admits of every conceivable variety of glazed surface.' His own glasshouse was followed by many others all over the country including the striking conservatory at Bretton Hall, Yorkshire, in 1827 which was erected by one of the main manufacturers of cast iron, W. & D. Bailey (Plate 66). It was 30 metres in diameter and 18 metres high. It was dismantled shortly afterwards in 1832.

Joseph Paxton has survived as the greatest exponent of cast-iron glasshouses. His Great Exhibition Building of 1851 ensures his place in

66. **BRETTON HALL**, West Yorkshire
    1827

history. But, this was a development from his earlier experience in his design for the Great Conservatory at Chatsworth (Plate 67), which took four years to construct and which was completed in 1840. Paxton used for this Great Stove, as it was then called, the ridge-and-furrow construction that Loudon had invented. Paxton and Loudon had much respect for each other. Paxton forgave Loudon his first contact with him in the 1830s. Loudon, who always wrote what he felt to be true, had published a devastating criticism of the layout and management of the gardens at Chatsworth then in the care of an unknown gardener called Paxton. The Chatsworth Stove was about 30 metres wide by 85 metres long and 20 metres to its crown. It was built to house the largest tropical trees which could be imported and grown and the Duke of Devonshire used to take his guests through the building in their carriages. Indeed, it became so famous, attracting tens of thousands of visitors, that a special railway station had to be built to cater for them. One of its great successes was that its controlled environment, using sun power, permitted the giant water-lily, *Victoria Regia*, to be grown for the first time in England. Though the Stove was a great achievement, Paxton saw it as engineering to be set within the arboretum at Chatsworth where it could not conflict with the architecture of the great house. It was so neglected during the First World War that it had to be demolished in 1920. Half a century later Chatsworth had a new conservatory which was designed by G. A. Pearce RIBA and completed in 1970 (Plate 68). Though it does not compete in grandeur with its predecessor, it also reflects structural innovation. It is based on an earlier glasshouse, erected in the 1960s at

67. CHATSWORTH STOVE, Derbyshire
1840

68. CHATSWORTH PLANT HOUSE, Derbyshire
1970

69. GLASSHOUSES, Cheshunt, Hertfordshire
   c. 1960

Edinburgh, designed by the same architect. Chatsworth's new plant
house is formed from a thin portal frame which is supported from an
external suspension system. This creates an elegant structure which is
set on a sloping site in the vegetable gardens. It is divided into three
sections to provide different environmental conditions. It has a
minimum height of 3 metres to the eaves and 6 metres to the ridge. Its
tension cables from the aluminium frame make the building ornamental as well as functional.

The commercial glasshouse has become ubiquitous. It ranges from
the little glass shed in many a suburban garden to the serried rows of
narrow spans that can cover many hectares, as around Cheshunt in
Hertfordshire, photographed about 1960 (Plate 69). The problem of
commercial horticulture in northern climates is that sun power alone
cannot cosset the crops enough. Thus, the rows of glass are punctured
by small brick chimneys which provide artificial heat to keep the
warmth constant during the cold winters. In this, they repeat the technique of the old stoves of the sixteenth and seventeenth centuries, but
manual stoking gave way to pressure-jet oil furnaces. The reliance on
fossil fuels, as in other spheres, has created an economic crisis. Most of
the glasshouses at Cheshunt have been swept away and replaced by
other development. Only the most efficient, most intensive, commercial glasshouses can remain viable now that oil has become an expensive fuel. Vast acres of glass-covered ground, which are expensive in

buildings and maintainenace, can be profitable only when they are providing crops at a time or place when nature cannot do it out of doors.

Glasshouses *en masse* defy the normal definition of what is a farm building. But horticulture is an extension of normal crop production and glasshouses are a type of building. They have a wide range of functions, some common to farms, such as for potato chitting—that is for germinating seed potatoes. The example near Newport, Shropshire, was erected in the 1950s (Plate 70). Light is maintained at night by banks of fluorescent tubes.

70. POTATO CHITTING HOUSE, Newport, Salop
    1950s

Seed-beds can be forced by translucent materials other than glass, and plastic sheeting has become a common aid. Perforated sheeting was laid over 140 hectares of ridged early potato beds at the Limburgerhof Research Station in West Germany during the 1970s. The covering helps to provide warmth and humidity around the plants until lifted each May, the foliage pushing the plastic film upwards as it grows. This can lead to a harvest some three weeks earlier than normal. The distinction as to what is a 'building' is very blurred in agriculture. Further development has taken place in many parts of Europe including at Pwllcaerog, Dyfed (Plate 71) where 40 hectares of early potatoes were covered by plastic by 1980, being laid in February of that year.

The age of experiment in harnessed sun power is not over. The tower glasshouse may yet take its place as a legitimate heir to Loudon. The first tower was erected in 1963 at the School of Gardeners at Langenlois in Austria. It was 10 metres high. It proved so successful that one 41 metres high was erected the following year in Vienna at the International Horticultural Exhibition. The tower was 9 metres in diameter

71. PLASTIC FILM laid over potato beds

and its tower contained a spiral conveyor 240 metres long by 4.5 metres wide, run in three loops to provide six columns of plants, each 38 metres high. The conveyor holds supports for 35,000 plant pots or, if seedling containers are fixed, 200,000 plants. The 'continuous flow technique' for pot plants was invented to apply industrial techniques to horticulture. Plants on conveyors seem to be a logical development in glasshouse technology. Horizontal walkways between seed-beds are inefficient both in the use of space and for working posture. Bringing the plant to the worker at the height comfortable for cultivation creates the possibility of flow-line production. Continuous movement of the conveyor, spiralling within a vertical column, saves both ground space and, more important, means each plant will receive the same total quantity of sunlight. All plants return to the worker for inspection at prescribed intervals. With high plant density in the limited volume, the internal climate is easier and cheaper to maintain so that ventilating, heating, lighting and watering are more efficient. A top speed of 4 metres per minute, which permits one complete revolution every 60 minutes and which also allows for adequate attendance time, makes control and selection of plants for marketing easy to manage by one man.

Several towers have been built and at least one experiment has been made in the United Kingdom. Unfortunately, such mechanical plant is expensive and with the increase in fuel costs it is unlikely that the development will be used extensively at present. Nevertheless, plastic-covered fields and automated glasshouses are likely eventually to be commonplace as food production becomes more intensive.

General references

1. G. F. Chadwick, *The Works of Sir Joseph Paxton*, Architectural Press, 1961.
2. J. Gloag, *Mr Loudon's England*, Oriel, 1970.
3. J. Hix, *The Glass House*, Phaidon Press, 1973.
4. R. McGrath and A. C. Frost, *Glass in Architecture and Decoration*, Architectural Press, 1961.

72. TOWER GLASSHOUSE

Gravity Power

Farmers have always used gravity to assist them both on the land and in the farmstead. Irrigation is a particular use of gravity. It was used in Egypt; it was practised by the Elizabethans with a system of dykes, dams and sluices which fed from and drained back to a river. Rowland Vaughan in 1589 called it 'wetshod waterworks'. Later it became known as 'floating the meadows'. Some farm buildings used contours to provide a split-level design. Others were constructed with a loft on the principle that what was carried up could tumble down again when required. This was a form of conservation of energy since loading a loft could be done in 'slack' time.

The Victorians in particular used gravity to assist farmwork. Though previous generations may have made use of gravity, it was the Victorian designers who exploited sites on great or model farms to gain maximum advantage of ground slopes. One of the most ambitious of these was erected in 1852 for the Earl of Radnor at Coleshill in Berkshire (now absorbed into Oxfordshire). This layout was designed by a London architect, George Lamb (Plates 73 and 74). The new steading was set out within an area of some 1.5 hectares (150×100 metres) along a slope of nearly 15 metres. This was adjusted, on cut-and-fill basis, to form a split-level design with a 4-metre change of level at the main run of barns across the site. The upper level contained a rick-yard enclosure, the ricks being carted into the first floor of the barn for threshing, sacking

73. COLESHILL MODEL FARM, Berkshire, plan and section 1852

74. COLESHILL MODEL FARM, bird's-eye view

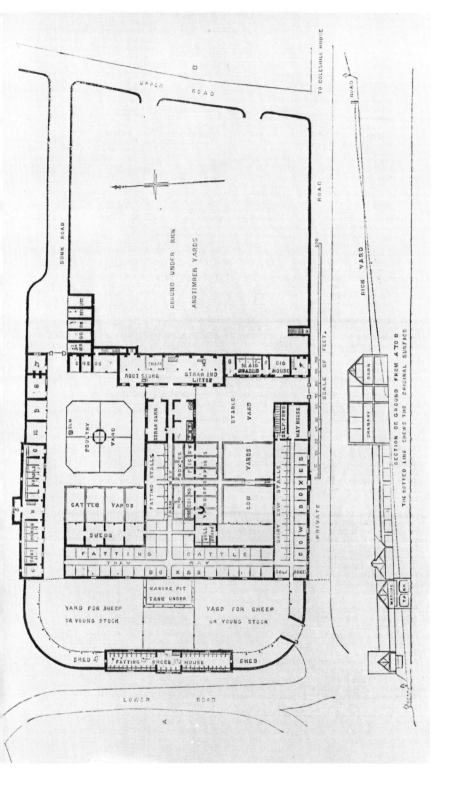

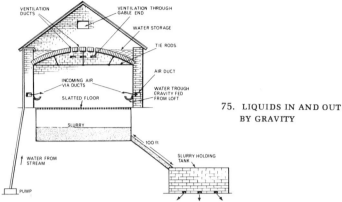

75. LIQUIDS IN AND OUT
BY GRAVITY

and weighing. Sacks were moved into the adjacent granary. They could be lowered through a trapdoor on to a wagon in the carriageway underneath. Alternatively, they could be discharged through shutes into a feed preparation room. The feed was taken into stock buildings in trucks run along tramways let into the feed passage's flooring. Chaff and straw, as well as roots, were dropped from the upper barn to the lower floor where a stone mill, a root-cutter and a straw-chopper could be used before distribution along the tramways. The change of level was used also to permit effluent from the livestock to percolate, via underfloor channels, to a large underfloor tank. The base of the latter was level with the lowest point of the site. These buildings were studied in 1980 by the Architects in Agriculture Group with regard to their past, present and future (see references).

The practice of having cattle on slatted floors was known early in the nineteenth century. Arranging that effluent could fall naturally between slats into a pit and then drain to a lower tank provided a major reduction in manual work (Plate 75). Liquids could seep via channels to help fertilize the land. In this particular case, pumped water was stored above a vaulted ceiling. It had to be pumped there but, as it was consumed, gravity kept the drinking bowls filled. The principle of tanks feeding bowls by gravity is still adopted in many livestock buildings.

76.
MILK COOLING
Upright and
swing stand
1900

77.
ALTON WATERMILL, Suffolk,
exterior. The mill showing
the projecting lucam at the
gable, and beyond it the
millhouse (see also Plates 84
to 87). The land, including
the mill site, was flooded in
the 1970s to form Alton
Water—the reservoir for
Ipswich. Mill and millhouse
were moved to the Museum
of East Anglian Life,
Stowmarket, Suffolk, in
1972

The principle of the milk cooling device sold by the Dairy Supply Company in 1900 (Plate 76) was still employed until modern refrigerated bulk tanks became the norm. Pails of milk were poured into a receiver, then trickled over chilled surface coolers to fill a churn. The cooler contained chilled water pumped from a fan chamber. More recently, it has been possible to pipe the milk direct from the cow to the cooler (Plate 138).

Granular materials, such as corn and feed, are easy to let flow from lofts. The old mills (Plates 77 and 78) worked on this basis, sacks being hoisted to the ridge level, via the lucam, then emptied into roof bins which funnelled the grain into a hopper which, in turn, trickled the

78. ALTON WATERMILL, Suffolk, stone floor. The mill in 1972, prior to being moved but having ceased working 1950, showing the grain chutes into the encased pair of stones. On the right is the sluice gate which, when raised, permitted water to pass along the trough and over the (overshot) water-wheel (see also Plate 85)

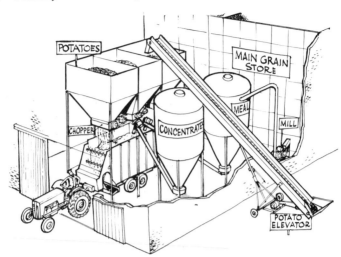

79. FEED MILL, Court Lodge, Appledore, Kent. Potatoes are elevated into
hoppers where they 'fall' into a chopper to 'fall' into a self-unloading
trailer. Similarly, meal is blown into bins where it 'falls' to the bottom to
be augered into the trailer to provide a mixed ration for livestock
1962

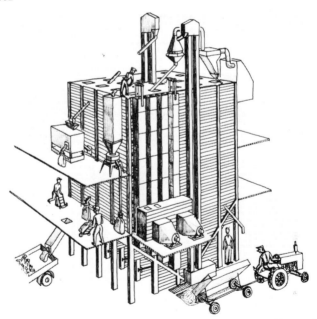

80. FEED MILL, LBF, Sweden. The complex plant—the 'nest' of bins—for
many mills, with their elevators, cyclones, blowers etc., still relies on
grain or meal 'falling' to a point where it can be sacked on a platform. The
sacks then slide down a chute on to a lorry
1962

81. GRAVITY FERTILIZER HANDLING, Rex Paterson's Farms, Basingstoke, Hampshire
1960

82. EXPERIMENTAL SILO WALLS
1974

grain on to the grinding stones. Modern grain and feed plant (Plates 79 and 80) still use gravity but, today, this is assisted by other mechanical conveyors.

Fertilizers can be handled in bulk (Plate 81). With a split-level transit store, they can be tipped into a bunker from which they can trickle through a damper into a tractor-drawn fertilizer spreader.

Grass can be kept (ensiled) in horizontal clamps for winter feed if it is not dried to form hay. Silage became popular during the 1960s. The clamps can be simple affairs, some 2 metres deep. The essential thing is that the grass should be compacted to squeeze out oxygen and moisture, then being kept airtight to prevent fermentation. Compaction is made by driving a tractor on top of the grass, particularly whilst filling the clamp. It is practical—and better since it improves compaction thereby reducing fermentation—to build the clamp 3 to 5 metres deep, but the higher the tractor goes, the greater the pressure on the walls of the clamp. Pressures can be held by retaining walls, but these tend to be expensive. Work at Shuttleworth College Farm, Bedfordshire, in 1971, under the direction of the National Institute of Agricultural Engineering, showed that a clamp 5.5 metres high was practical. Flexible, sprung walls of welded mesh, suspended from a steel cradle, with a pre-tensioned boom, and covered with reinforced PVC sheets recorded pressures that were 25 per cent less than those on rigid walls. Thus, the tractor pressure, plus the self-weight of the grass, together with sprung walls, become a sophisticated version of the use of gravity in the compression of grass. (For an account of the history of silage, see page 197.)

Water Power

The bladed wheel, turned by a stream, has a long history. Both the Greeks and the Romans used water power. John Reynolds in his study of *Windmills and Watermills* (Hugh Evelyn, 1970) has covered the subject in great detail. Water power was used to raise water to above river level or to grind corn. There are several Greek references to corn mills in the first century BC and, at the same time, the Romans termed them hydraula, as did Vitruvius in his great work of ten books on *De Architectura*. Vitruvius described the construction of the machinery in some detail both for raising water and for corn. He may have invented the mechanism suitable for powerful rivers like the Tiber. A century later, Palladius had called them *mola aquaria*. It is probable that water-wheels and, possibly, corn mills existed in Persia several centuries before Christ. What is known as the Greek mill survived in Persia and became a great power source a millennia later when the Roman Empire had disintegrated.

The Greek mill was distinctive in that it was powered from a horizontal water-wheel. The great dam at Band-e-Emir was constructed before the Normans came to Britain. Its reservoir, the leat, powered over thirty corn mills settled around its sluices. Only about a dozen survive. Elizabeth Beazley has described this remarkable cluster of mills.[1] The principle is that a small volume of water is directed under pressure to turn the horizontal wheel which then turns a vertical shaft. The latter passes through a fixed lower stone to turn the upper millstone. The base of the shaft, the great axle, rest with an iron shaft on to a sole plate or tree. The tree acts as a lever since its position can be finely adjusted by moving the lightning rod which is pivoted from the grinding room over

[1] 'Greek Mills in Iran', *Architectural Review*, 1977, pp. 311–13.

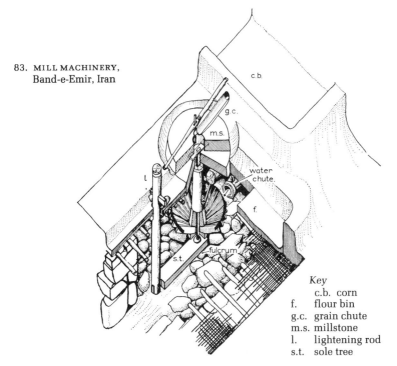

83. MILL MACHINERY,
Band-e-Emir, Iran

Key
c.b. corn
f. flour bin
g.c. grain chute
m.s. millstone
l. lightening rod
s.t. sole tree

the wheelhouse. Thus, the distance apart of the millstones can be adjusted by the miller, by remote control, to vary the fineness of flour produced. This type of mill, which is unusual in northern Europe (except the Shetlands) is common throughout much of the Mediterranean and, via Portuguese and Spanish settlers, in Peru and South Africa. It may have been used on minor rivers in Britain but such references as exist do not make this clear.

The vertical water-wheel, the *mola aquaria* of the Romans, spread throughout Europe in the later stages of their Empire. By the time the Domesday Book was compiled in 1087, well over 2000 mills were recorded within a wide range of ownership and capacities for grinding. Milling, though closely related to farming, has been mainly set apart from it. Trajan, at the turn of the first century AD, had founded the College of Pistors in Rome to regulate the craft of milling and baking. But, by the time of the Norman Conquest, the pistor was no longer the miller, being confined mainly to the task of baking. Saxon millers had been men of property and position, thus often working as farmers. But, already, some instances occurred where tenants were forced to grind at the manorial mill. In medieval times, the manorial or the leased mill became the norm. As Chaucer's *Canterbury Tales* make clear, the miller was to become a detested person. He had great power and many were corrupt. The number of poultry he was permitted to keep was restricted so that he could not feed them on the grain deposited with him for grinding.

Many watermills were kept separate from the farm and they became a distinct feature of the landscape along rivers. The sufficiency of water in the river for power was a major issue in their siting, and it was frequently the subject of conflict in the manorial courts. A catchment area to hold water above the mill was essential on many rivers. When released, the head turned the wheel and the released water in time reached the leat to the next downstream mill where it would be impounded until there was sufficient head. Thus, there was a strict timetable for when the miller could operate his stones. Some could be forced to work unsocial hours. If a miller delayed operation, all the mills downstream would be delayed. In the eastern counties, where contours are gradual, a watermill might only be practical every two to five miles along the watercourse. It was a delicate social arrangement and misunderstandings could occur.

The siting of mills had to relate both to the watercourse and to access from the cornland. Some were closely related to farmland and were included with farmsteads. This was true particularly with manor farms. The development of gearing in the mill was related to the efficiency by which the power could be harnessed. In upland areas the water was taken over the top of the water-wheel on the 'overshot' principle. This was the most efficient technique, but in lowland districts the blades had to be reversed to permit power to be taken by an undershot thrust of water. The Rossett mill and millhouse complex (Plate 85) are dated 1661 and it is typical of the popular image of watermills. The buildings

PRIVY   HOUSE   MILL   OUTBUILDINGS

MILL   OUTBUILDINGS   CART SHED

84. OVERSHOT WATER-WHEEL, Stutton, Suffolk, delt. J. T. Sheridan

85. UNDERSHOT WATER-WHEEL, Rosett, Clwyd
Mid-1960s

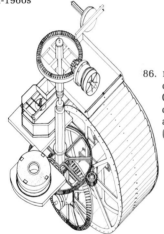

86. MILL MACHINERY, Stutton, Suffolk,
delt. J. T. Sheridan.
One pair of stones is omitted,
one pair shown uncased
and one pair properly encased
(see also Plate 78)

were redundant in the 1960s and have since been converted to other uses. The Alton watermill (Plate 84), millhouse and farmstead, near Stutton, Suffolk were also made redundant after the Second World War and ceased grinding early in the 1950s. The Holbrook had a series of watermills, including that to Alton Hall, spaced every two or three miles apart on its short course to the Suffolk coast. The mill is unusual in that its pond is filled from a canal, or leat, dug back over one mile to pick up a sufficient head for the overshot wheel, before the water drains back to its original brook. Since the mill is circa 1800, it is possible that French prisoners were used for the task. The original water-wheel was external to the building, as at Rossett, but was later enclosed within an extended structure.

The principle of the machinery (Plate 86) is that the water enters via a

87. ALTON MILL, Stutton, Suffolk, being dismantled 1972. The last rim of the water-wheel is being lifted out by crane. The cast-iron hurst frame which had carried two of the pairs of stones is still *in situ*, as is the pit-wheel. The main axle and shaft lie near the lorry

88. ALTON MILL, millhouse and cartshed, re-erected at Stowmarket,
Suffolk, 1974. Architect, John B. Weller

sluice over the wooden pentrough or penstock (see Plate 78) to turn the
water-wheel of 3.8 metres diameter. This turns the main axle which
turns the pit-wheel. This is meshed with the wallower, the small pinion
that turns the spur-wheel and then the main vertical shaft. The latter
operates the crown-wheel on the floor above—the sack floor—which
operates the subsidiary machinery via a series of drive shafts and drive
belts, including the main sack hoists. The crown-wheel, via special
stone nuts, turns the runner stones—in this case there are three pairs of
stones. The crown-wheel, also enclosed, can be used to drive any
low-powered machinery including normal small hammer-mills and
rollers. However, all mills are dust laden and corn dust can be explo-
sive, fired from minor sparks. Throughout history, mills have been
prone to destruction by fire.

Prior to flooding the Stutton/Holbrook valley to form a new reservoir
for Ipswich, the mill, millhouse and cartshed were dismantled and
re-erected at the Museum of East Anglian Life at Stowmarket, Suffolk
(Plates 87 and 88).

Michael Menzies, concerned that flails wasted corn, invented a
threshing machine in 1732. It was powered by a water-wheel which
turned a beam to operate a row of flails. Three were erected in East
Lothian which were inspected by the Honourable Society of Improvers
in the Knowledge of Agriculture in Scotland. Straw was first hand-
flailed. The new machine then threshed out a quarter peck of good grain

to twelve bolts of straw and one man did the work of six while the axle cranked the beam with thirty revolutions each minute along a line of sheaves spread on benches. The invention did not succeed because the velocity of the water power broke the flails.

Watermills fell into disuse in the 1950s and only a few still worked commercially in the 1970s. Health standards had made stone-ground flour suspect unless supervision is of good order, and water authorities charge for the 'use' of water over a mill-wheel even though it is difficult to show this really is the 'extraction' of water on which they base their charge. Milling, thus, can become uneconomic. But stone-ground flour for quality baking—let alone grist for livestock—is regaining its reputation and there could be a revival of watermills to meet the problem of high-cost fossil fuels. In addition, secondary-powered equipment might again be used both on the farm and for some rural industries.

General reference

R. Bennett, and J. Elton, *Watermills and Windmills* (*History of Cornmilling*, vol. 2), 1899 (reprinted EP Publishing, 1973).

Wind Power

Power from the wind, as the popular song states, should be 'free as air'. This has been disputed: first as a breach of feudal soke laws; today as a breach of development rights. Throughout history, the use of 'free' power which is available at any exposed site has required special permits from the state.

The origin of the windmill is unknown. Vitruvius, who described contemporary innovations under the Roman Empire a score of years before Christ, only referred to 'spiritalia' which were wind-driven machines producing 'organ sounds'. For the next thousand years, all other references to wind power remain obscure, but they are unlikely to mean the mechanical use of wind energy. In the Islamic world, in the centuries immediately before the Christian millennium, wind sails were added to the horizontal mills powered normally by water. Such innovations were to assist land irrigation and water supplies.

It seems that windmills for corn evolved in the twelfth century in various parts of Gothic Europe. There are several references at the end of that century. The clearest and most dramatic, perhaps, is in the *Chronicle of Joceylin de Brakelond*, almoner to the largest abbey in Europe, that for Bury St. Edmunds in Suffolk, He wrote in 1191 concerning the anger of Abbot Samson at the illegal mill built on glebe lands by his dean: 'We said withal there was a terrible flash of anger in Samson: witness his address to old Herbert the Dean who in a too thrifty manner has erected a windmill for himself on his glebe lands at Haberdon . . . "By God's face I will not eat bread till that fabric be torn in pieces. Thou art an old man and shouldst have known that neither the king nor his justiciary dare change aught within the liberties without consent of abbot and convent; and thou has presumed on such a thing! I tell thee it will not be without damage to my mills for the townsfolk will go to thy mill and grind their corn at their own good pleasure." ' This was the truth of the matter. As with watermills, use of natural power by all and sundry would undermine the restrictive and valuable practice of milling by licence. And wind was even more freely available than water. Water-milling was held by franchise under soke deeds of feudal law.

Mills, called 'molendinum ad ventum' by Joceylin, became common-place throughout northern Europe during the thirteenth century. The battle for freedom of use of wind was fought out in the courts during that century. Judicial records show that the principle that water-power franchise should include wind power was quickly established. There was no disputing the summary of the Tudor legal situation made by Chief Justice Fitzherbert in his *Boke of Surveying* of 1538: 'A windmill whereunto all the lord's tenants are bound to grind all their corn and malt.' Since milling was a restrictive trade, granted by licence and worked by specialist millers, and since windmills, because of their particular nature, were best set apart on exposed ground, it is no wonder they were not a normal feature of the farmstead. Nevertheless, by the eighteenth century, when feudal rights had been broken, any serious study of agricultural husbandry would consider the mechanics of mil-ling. For example, Alexander Mabyn Bailey edited *Mechanical Machines and Implements of Husbandry* in 1782. He presented several accounts of mill machinery including an engraving of the beautiful model for a smock mill (Plate 89). This was made to a scale of $1\frac{1}{2}$ inches to 1 foot on an internal floor base measuring 2 foot square. The method by which the vane and sails could turn the great platform at the base is shown clearly. Grain was crushed on the platform by eight posts which rose and fell using the same power. This was not a common technique and the model was aimed to propagate new principles as 'Approved and adopted by the Society for the Encouragement of Arts, Manufac-tures and Commerce'. The first three of eleven books were on agricul-ture. Bailey was registrar to the Society.

The evolution and mechanics of the post, smock and tower mills, together with other variant forms, have been described fully by John Reynolds (see Bibliography). Windmills became a distinctive feature of landscapes in many parts of the world, particularly Europe, Islam and China. Many, particularly the great wheels of Persia, were for irrigation or land drainage and, naturally, were sited in the open landscape. Most windmills for this purpose were replaced by electric pumps earlier this century. The drainage mill has almost disappeared in advanced

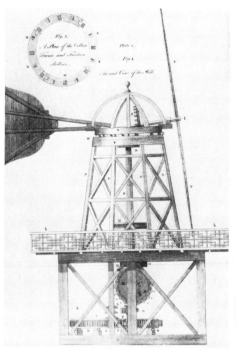

89. MR EVER'S MILL. 1782   90. HERRINGFLEET SMOCK MILL, Suffolk

agricultural regions. One of the last in East Anglia, at Herringfleet (Plate 90), was saved in the mid-1970s to become a monument to a vanished age. This mid-nineteenth-century smock mill, with its boat-shaped cap and its hooded scoop-wheel at its side, was typical of marshland and fen. Herringfleet was one of several drainage mills used on the flood plain of the River Waveney in Suffolk.

Most of the outlying windmills were for corn. Usually, the miller had his own house, his orchard garden and his work-sheds set around his mill. Many have been destroyed following the Industrial Revolution. Some are now preserved as monuments, but now that stone-ground flour is seen to provide a more wholesome bread, a few have been restored for milling. Sometimes, the windmill created a sizeable, associated industry around it, producing a complex of courtyard buildings similar to a farmstead. The beautiful tower of Skidby Mill, near Beverley, in Humberside was erected in 1821 (Plate 92). It was still working in the 1960s when it became a museum. The brickwork is tarred and it has a fine cap and fantail similar to that at Terling. Around the base are granaries, stores, cartsheds and horseboxes. Many millers also became merchants rather than farmers. Thus, milling was associated with industry rather than with the land.

91. TERLING SMOCK MILL, Essex. A majestic 18th-century survivor, with its
conical cap and fantail, already patched with corrugated iron in 1955 and
falling into disuse following the post-war depression of a traditional, rural
industry

92. SKIDBY TOWER MILL, Humberside

The windmill has had a limited function in the farmstead. Arthur Young illustrated the integration of windmill with milk production in his famous *Annals of Agriculture* (Vol. 33), published in 1799. It showed a circular layout for a threshing yard (Plates 93 and 94). The design is remarkable for a number of reasons. The corn stacks are wheeled so that they can be trundled to the windmill where they can be threshed. Not shown in the sketch, the mill can be coupled to the granary and chaff house. Meal and straw can be used for the encircling ring of cows in their simple monopitch shelter. The ensuing dung can be raked back to form a dunghill which, later, can be spread on the surrounding corn lands when ploughed. Obviously, this is an ingenious, labour-saving layout which makes full use of the fact that the windmill needed to be on exposed farmland—indeed taking stock to where the corn is ground. Arthur Young criticized the conventional farmstead in his *Annals* (p. 497): 'In the farm buildings of former times we cannot look for such designs; but in modern ones I own I never see, but with regret, here a granary, and there a chaff-house; a threshing-mill; scattered stalls, stables, cow-houses, and I know not what; with or without huge barns; and if you ask why any one of them is placed precisely where you find it, no reason can be given for three-fourths of the arrangement.' The circular threshing yard was his answer to this lament. He described his layout with loving care (*Annals*, pp. 488—98):

The frames on which the stacks are built are of wood and fixed, like a

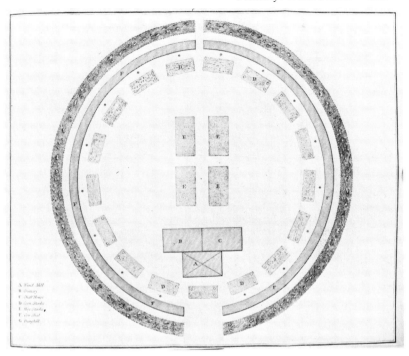

93. CIRCULAR THRESHING YARD, plan

94. CIRCULAR THRESHING YARD, view, Arthur Young, *Annals of Agriculture*, 1799

Norfolk moveable barn, on wheels; which wheels turn in a fixed circular groove or road of wood or cast iron. ... the power applied to the threshing-mill is at hand, and applicable also to this work, it may be used ... the threshing-mill being fixed on the side of the circular road admits the stacks being drawn to it, where a shed is erected, under which the stack rests. This shed (a roof on four posts) is not represented in the plate. ... the stack is there unthatched, and the corn thrown at once to the mill, without for a moment being exposed to rain, and without any labour of men, or horses, or carriages to move it. The straw, as fast as threshed, is piled on the stack frame last cleared, or any other way disposed of. Adjoining the mill there is a granary, and a wheel and pulley may easily be added, for drawing up the sacks from the spout which fills them from the dressing-machine. ...

A. in the circular ground pit, is the position of the mill, on one side of which is the circular road, the path of the stacks; on the other, and contiguous, but below the sails, are the granary and chaff-house.

B. is the granary, into which the corn is hoisted, as ground and dressed by the machinery, and containing also the meal of barley, or pease and beans, if there is apparatus for grinding them, in order to feed cattle; also for oilcake, with a breaking cylinder, turned by the power of wind, in order for feeding of cattle.

C. is the receptacle for chaff: and the site of a cutter, to work also by a cog-wheel from the first movement.

D. the corn stacks.

E. the hay stacks.

F. are the cattle sheds. ... no limit to any, as it is only proposed to connect them (whatever the plan of stalls may be) in the most convenient manner with the hay, corn, straw, oilcake etc:. By means of a projection at the height of five feet in the wall, against the heads of the cattle, the hay may be put at once into the racks. ... between the line of the stacks and the wall of the cattle-shed, there may be just enough space left for a one horse cart to pass, to unload turnips or cabbages, or potatoes. ... the circular shed for cattle should contain not only the fatting beasts, but also the cows, young cattle, ox and horse teams. ... the area in the centre need not be lost for if paled in a hay-rack *forming a part of the pale* and covered by a low shed, the whole is well adapted to the use of a standing sheep-fold. ... the dunghill is in the outward circumference of the several circles. ... the site of the whole system is on the elevation of a very gentle knowle or hill.

Like Young, Loudon had to consider windmills as an essential part of his *Encyclopædia of Cottage, Farm and Villa Architecture* of 1833. He took much further the concept of integration of milling with the farmstead. He produced a number of model farm layouts for different locations. One was considered suitable for 100 acres (40 hectares) of land which could be cultivated on the 'Norfolk System' and included 'farm house, farmery, and flour mill driven by wind' (p. 473) (Plate 95). The farmhouse was luxurious for the period, including parlour, kitchen, counting house, store room, pantry, brewhouse, dairy, and six bedrooms (two of which had fires). The farm layout was designed by Wm. Thorold, an architect and engineer of Norwich. It was considered suitable for 80 arable acres and 20 grass acres.

The mill, which included Cubitt's patent sails, would have cost £1000 but could grind each week some 20 quarters (about 250 kilo-

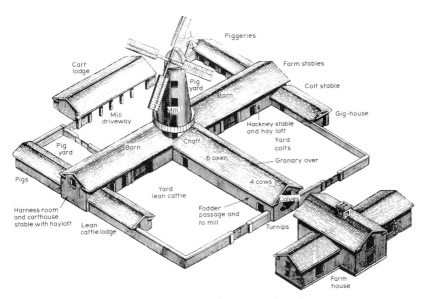

95. NORFOLK SYSTEM FARMSTEAD, Loudon's *Encyclopædia*, 1833

grammes) of flour for sale and 10 quarters for local grist to the livestock. There was a special attachment to permit horse power to be used when winds were not available. And, most important, the mill could also take attachments for threshing, for hay-cutting, for drawing (husking), as well as for rolling trefoil, clover and small seeds, and for pumping. The mill is set over the main barns and its by-products go directly to the stock yards. Even the mill offal was fed to the pigs. Nothing was wasted.

It was not until the early to mid-nineteenth century that windmills began to be closely integrated with traditional farmstead buildings. Loudon showed how it was a logical development. But, at the same time, steam power, and later diesel and electrical, began to oust natural—and rather intermittent—sources of power. Farm windmills, except for pumping water, had a short period of popularity.

It is possible that wind power could again become an important element on the farm. This could be for a number of functions. One of the most dramatic revivals was attempted in the mid-1970s at Efford Experimental Horticultural Station in Hampshire. The principle developed for heating glasshouses was akin to that in the diagram in Plate 96. The tower required is 13 metres high carrying rotating, glass-fibre blades of 18 metres diameter capable of 120 rpm. These turn a shaft and the mechanical energy generated is converted to heat energy via a hydraulic pump which squeezes oil through a small hole. Hot oil is insulated and conveyed to a calorifier which, in turn, is used to heat water circuits in the glasshouses. The intention was that up to 150,000 kilowatts a year would be generated, extracting about 40 per cent of the wind's power—that is proportional to the square of the rotor diameter.

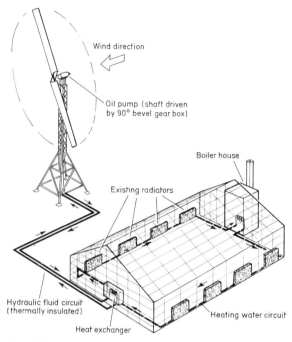

Wind direction

Oil pump (shaft driven by 90° bevel gear box)

Boiler house

Existing radiators

Hydraulic fluid circuit (thermally insulated)

Heating water circuit

Heat exchanger

96. WINDMILLS FOR GLASSHOUSES

The site is only moderately windy, averaging 5 metres per second, whereas any site averaging 6 metres per second would generate 70 per cent more energy. At Efford, there are over 1000 square metres of glasshouses, which could be heated partly from wind and, when this is slack, by oil. The experiment was not concluded.

The technology of modern windmills has changed from that used in traditional constructions. Modern wind power comes from aerogenerators, aerofoils and other derivatives of aerodynamic engineering. Their implication for food production has not yet been realized. Their effect on the future landscape has not been discussed—though they do require planning permission when above 12 metres in height.

General references

1. R. Bennett and J. Elton, *Watermills and Windmills* (History of Corn-milling, Vol. 2), 1899 (reprinted EP Publishing, 1973).
2. S. Freese, *Windmills and Millwrighting*, David & Charles, 1971.
3. R. Wailes, *The English Windmill*,& Kegan Paul, 1954.

SECONDARY (MUSCULAR) POWER SOURCES

Manual Power

Men have always worked the land by the sweat of their brow—at least until recent times. John Ball inspired the peasants to revolt in 1381 by the image of:

> When Adam delved and Eve span
> who was then the gentleman?

This conveyed accurately that agricultural life was for those who toiled, and only the teamwork of the whole family made it practical. At the same time, farmwork has had an aura of pleasurable toil and a close affinity with nature. The concept of pastoral arcadia haunts urban man, lost as it is within the Garden of Eden. Raymond Williams in his *The Country and the City* (Chatto & Windus, 1973) has argued clearly that, looking for the golden age, our vision is held by an endless perspective, no period really being 'golden': 'When we moved back in time, consistently directed to an earlier and happier rural England, we could find no place, no period, in which we could seriously rest.' In reality, both in the field and in the steading, man has made every attempt possible to develop sources of power to free him from manual work. Delving and spinning may be pleasurable as short-term recreation but purgatory when forming the basis of a life support system.

Simple, mass-produced tools are what the farmer needs. Their history is that of man's evolution. The flint axehead and the bone needle introduced centuries of innovation. In the fifth century BC, the Chinese were mass-producing cast-iron sickle blades 325 millimetres long from twin iron moulds (Plate 97). Two millennia later similar blades were still cutting corn in many parts of the world. The illustration of hand reaping and binding and flailing in the *Canticum Canticorum*, pub-

97. CHINESE SICKLE-BLADE MOULD
c. 5th century BC

lished in 1455, shows the same type of sickle blade (Plate 98). The monks, blessed though they might be, laboured hard in the field, whilst others pounded the grain with their pestle after it had been sieved. In their shelter is the book of hours for their devotion and the mead for their refreshment.

98. MEDIEVAL CORN HARVEST, *Canticum Canticorum*, 1455

William Long, in his study of the development of farm mechanization, stressed the extent of hard, manual work on the seventeenth century farm: 'The farmer relied on hand tools for cultivating, harvesting, and barn and yard work. There was a variety of forks, described as hay, pike, half-pike, pitch, dung, dock, iron, and gripes. Other tools were shovels, spades, hacks, and gavelocks ... the seed bed has to be done by hand with the help of a moll ... the grain after threshing was dressed with a window cloth (winding or winnow cloth). The grain was finally bagged up into sacks or pokes. Sieves and riddles occur fairly frequently; there is some indication that each class of corn had its own size of riddle.... Dairy equipment was usually valued in considerable detail. Most farms had either a churn or a cheese press and many had both.'

Except for the ox-drawn plough, there was little relief from the need for every task to be done by hand both in the field and the steading. Joseph Blagrave published his *Epitome of the Whole Art of Husbandry* in 1669. The frontispiece illustrates clearly in its ten panels what Long

99. (left) FRONTISPIECE, Joseph Blagrave, *Epitome of the Whole Art of Husbandry*, 1669

100. (right) FRONTISPIECE, John Worlidge, *Husbandry*, 1694

has described (Plate 99). Oxen plough, harrow and cart, whilst the field worker plods along using his switch. Other men broadcast seed, plant orchard trees, make hurdles, collect honey, extract teeth from the ox, scythe and stook corn. Only the fisherman seems to work without effort.

A generation later, in 1668, John Worlidge wrote his *Systima Agricul-turæ—or Ye Mistery of Husbandry*. He published a second volume in 1694, with the help of one 'I.W.', Gent., which considered *British Vineyards and Cider*. The frontispiece shows a typical two-man cider press apparently worked by the sons of the prosperous yeoman farmer. In the background, horses pull the plough because oxen were beginning to be shunned by the wealthier farmers. On the newly ploughed land, seed is broadcast. The farm is in good order since the ravages of the Civil War were beginning to be forgotten in the new prosperity.

Threshing. The corn harvest was one of the most important stages in the farming calendar. Throughout history, the harvest supper with its harvest lord, or the harvest blessing, has been a key festival of thanksgiving when the barns were full. But, even as the corn was brought to the steading, another manual task began. Threshing to get the grain from the sheaves is a long, hard task and the implement to do this, the flail, hardly changed from biblical until mid-Victorian times and even then it continued in use on poorer farms. The flail was not finally ousted steam threshing or other mechanical devices until the 1920s in Buckinghamshire and it continued to be used on remoter farms well into the 1930s.

As Chronicles (I, chapter xxi) relate, David set up an altar on the threshing-floor of Ornan the Jebusite so that Israel might be spared from the pestilence that had stricken his people. And, being successful in this atonement, on the site of the altar David instructed his son, Solomon, to build the greatest temple ever known. Threshing was not done indoors. The threshing-floor was prepared ground, level or sloping slightly from the centre and beaten hard, on which the flails could thrash the straw. The space marked out might be some thirty to forty paces, depending on the crop, each man needing a clear radius in which to flail. Deuteronomy (chapter xxv) records that oxen were sometimes used: 'Thou shalt not muzzle the ox when he treadeth out the corn.' (See frontispiece.) The Romans had a mobile, heavy wood platform as a threshing-floor mounted on rollers, known as the *tribulum*, which was dragged by oxen.

The threshing-floor became a special place, constructed to well-known lore to provide a good surface. Philip Wright in his *Old Farm Implements* (Black, 1961) quotes one of his local farmers, a former Essex parson, Revd. W. L. Rham, who specified a good floor in the mid-nineteenth century: 'The soil is taken out to the depth of six to eight inches or more, and if the subsoil is moist a layer of dry sand or gravel is laid at the bottom three or four inches thick, and trod smooth and level. A mixture is made of clay or loam and sand with water to the consistency of common building mortar; to which is added some chalk or pounded shells or gypsum. Chaff, cow-dung and bullocks' blood are added and the whole is well worked up together. A coat of this is laid on the prepared bottom with a trowel, about an inch thick and allowed to dry. Another coat is added and the cracks filled up carefully. This is repeated until the desired thickness is produced. When it begins to harden, the whole is well-rammed with a heavy wooden rammer and every crack filled up, so as to give it the appearance of a uniform solid body. This is left to harden slowly and in a short time becomes sufficiently hard to be used.' Similar specifications exist for threshing-floors in medieval times. In richer farmsteads, the threshing-floor would be of smooth pegged oak boards or granite or other hard stone flags. Thomas Hardy in *Far From the Madding Crowd* described Bathsheba Everdene's barn as having 'a wood threshing floor in the centre, formed of thick oak, black with age and polished by the beating of flails for many generations, till it had grown as rich in hue as the stateroom floors of an Elizabethan mansion'.

101. TISBURY TITHE BARN, Wiltshire, re-thatching in 1971

102.
WHITEHOUSE FARM,
Woodbastwick,
Norfolk
c. 1965

With the uncertain weather conditions of northern Europe, the barn, with its indoor threshing-floor set between the stacking areas for the sheaves, became a feature of the landscape. One-tenth of the harvest went to the abbey or the manor church, and the great tithe barns are magnificent architecture. Tisbury tithe barn, which belonged to the fifteenth-century Shaftesbury nunnery, is nearly 60 metres long and it is reputed to be the largest surviving in England. Once it was stone tiled. Later it was thatched with wheat straw, then by reed straw when re-thatched in 1971. J. E. Manners has described how it took 130,000 bundles of Norfolk reed of 750 millimetres girth, weighing 270 tonnes, to cover the 1200 square metres of thatch to a depth of some 300 millimetres. The ridge is of sedge, since this is more supple. This example is interesting in that it shows how manual labour is also associated with farm by-products. Though the roof should last seventy years with some maintenance, it took a five-man team four months to do the work.[1] In arable areas, even the humbler farm had its own small corn barn, often following the general pattern of the tithe barns.

Threshing creates considerable dust and the method for removing the latter, the winnowing, is important in old and new barn designs. Threshing used to take place in the midstrey, that is the area between the stacks, which normally has tall barn doors to each flank. When open, the cross wind helps to blow the chaff and dust clear of the work area. John Keats expressed how this was a common farm experience in his famous evocation *To Autumn*:

> Who hath not seen thee oft amid thy store?
>   Sometimes whoever seeks abroad may find
> Thee sitting careless on a granary floor,
>   Thy hair soft-lifted by the winnowing wind.

The full-height doors permit the great ox-carts to pull into the building to off-load the sheaves. Since the oxen cannot back, it is important that they have a through way across the barn (see also Plate 198).

103. FLAIL THRESHING. C. 1900   104. FLAIL, detail of joint

The flail had many other local names, including drashel, stick-and-a-half, frail, nile, thrail, Joseph-and-Mary. Essentially, they were of the same basic design. There was a hand shaft, usually of ash but sometimes of hazel, and a swingle, which means a half, of hawthorn. The centre swivel would be of green ash attached by eel skin or, when that was not

[1] J. E. Manners, 'Thatching England's Biggest Barn', *Country Life*, 18 November 1971, pp. 1403–4.

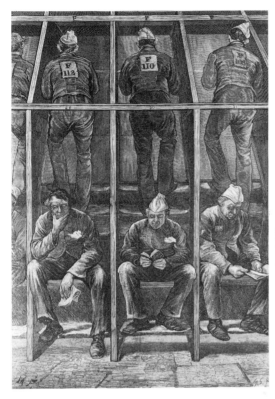

105.
TREADMILL, Clerkenwell
House of Correction
1874

available, by leather, thonged together with cowhide. Men normally worked in pairs and could thresh at thirty strokes per minute and up to 12 bushels (about 450 litres) of wheat each day. In many cases, flailing was done by contractors who moved from farm to farm. Threshing by flail was not without waste. Attempts were made to mechanize flail beating in the eighteenth century by use of water power (page 103).

Watermills for grinding grain were commonplace (page 100), but the treadmill was used by teams of men for the same purpose. This was quite common practice in the nineteenth century as the example in Plate 105 from the *Illustrated London News* for 1874 makes clear.

Milking. Milking the cow twice a day was a manual chore usually reserved for women. All that was required was a pail and, preferably, a stool. It could take place anywhere and was often done in the open. Hand milking was normal practice well into the 1930s. The rough conditions on many a remote farm are shown in the farmyard milking at Felin Newydd in Cardiganshire around 1897 (Plate 106).

Attempts were made to improve working conditions in the cowshed.

106. HAND MILKING. 1897

107. IMPROVED LONDON COWSHED. 1894

A book on *Dairy Farming* by J. F. Sheldon published by Cassell in 1894 showed the interior of the 'Improved London Cow-shed' (Plate 107). Cows lived at comfortable stalls in an airy barn. Feeding at their stalls was made less onerous since daily rations of cattle cake and of hay could be trundled into the building from the store along a trackway for the barrow. Bedding and muck were still handled by pitchfork and rake. Milk was carried away in the cowgirl's panniers slung from her yoke.

The hygienic cowshed appealed to the more prosperous farmer and to the Milk Regulations which first came in during 1885. However, the same amount of manual effort is required, and the stool is unchanged from time-honoured design. The open pail has become a bucket with a lid to keep the milk clean when carried. Milk, stored and cooled in churns, had to be taken every day to a place for collection. In winter, with impassable farm roads, this could be by sledge—another hard task.

108. SCALING HILL FARM, Whitby, North Yorkshire. Winter 1935

The dream of mechanized milking was a preoccupation of the Victorians. An early machine was imported from America in 1862 and shown in the *Illustrated London News* (Plate 109). It was a strange contraption with the teats held by four elastic tubes linked to an alternative exhaust and reservoir of air created when two handles were quickly turned to create a vacuum. It could milk at a rate of a gallon (4.5 litres) a minute. The Murchland was inspected at work on farms by experts from the Highland and Agricultural Society who gave it their approval.

A Danish machine, patented by Jems Neilson, was imported by the Newark-on-Trent firm, W. N. Nicholson, in 1892 when it was illustrated in the *Journal of the Royal Agricultural Society of England* (Plate 110). Suction was obtained by a pressure exerted by two pairs of indiarubber cushions, which alternated from each side, pressing first on the upper and then on the lower part of the teats. This simulated hand milking.

109. MURCHLAND MILKING MACHINE. 1862

110. NEILSON'S MILKING MACHINE. 1892

111. PROCESSING MILK. 1832

The eccentric movement was operated by a chain and crank handle suspended from a cradle across the cow's back. The cow looks surprised and the machine was not very popular with the operator either since it took as much effort to turn the handle as to hand milk. The transition to modern pulsator milking machines was a long process (pages 162 and 176).

The farmhouse dairy, facing north or east with slatted windows, is a feature of rural England. The three-bay medieval house had parlour and kitchen at either side of the main stack, with the dairy beyond the kitchen as the third bay. A typical dairy was illustrated by Taylor Jeffreys in his book of 1832 on *The Farm—A New Account of Rural Tools and Produce* (Plate 111). All the manual tools for milk are shown, with the yoke hanging at the door, the pail, the skimming bowls, the

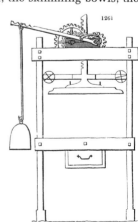

112. MR OGILVIE'S CHEESE PRESS
1830s

churn, the press and all the other equipment giving an air of cool efficiency. The walls are whitewashed and there is an attempt at good hygiene. The barrel-churn was 'new invented' in 1750 according to William Ellis in his *County Housewife's Companion* written in that year.

The cheese press and the churn, as William Long had written, were highly regarded. The cheese press was often 'improved' to suit local conditions. It became an early tool for urban manufacture. Loudon, in his *Encyclopædia* of 1839, illustrated the press designed by Mr. Ogilvie at Mere in Cheshire and manufactured in cast iron at Shotts Ironworks for 65 shillings. Pressure could easily be regulated from $1\frac{1}{2}$ to $2\frac{1}{2}$ tons by a system of wheel, pinion, lever and weight.

Barn work. Innovation of mechanical aids in the barn developed throughout the eighteenth century. These reflected the need to process crops to keep pace with improvements in cultivation. Elizabethan husbandry had greatly extended the practice of 'up-and-down' farming. This was a form of crop rotation in which fields were alternately ploughed up for corn and put down for grass. Thus, practices associated with medieval strip-fields began to end. As the seventeenth century progressed, new 'improved' grass seeds of clover and sainfoin became the norm. Land was drained and irrigated by 'floating', that is by channelling water through the subsoil by sequences of ditches along the contours. Turnips, made famous by Lord 'Turnip' Townshend in Norfolk, extended the rotational system. They also made it possible to feed livestock during the long winter months. Therefore, new stock buildings were required.

If there is to be a focus for the start of mechanization in farming, probably the name of Jethro Tull (1674–1741) should be chosen. He came from Basildon, in Berkshire, and qualified as a barrister and played the church organ. Looking at the latter gave him the idea that pipes could move seed and he invented his seed-drill in 1701. Drilling and hoeing was the basis of his philosophy which, since he was a prophet ahead of his time, revolutionized agriculture a generation or two later. He published his philosophy in 1733 as *The Horse-Hoeing Husbandry: or an essay on the principles of tillage and vegetation; wherein is shown a sort of vineyard culture into the corn-fields in order to increase their product and diminish the common experience; by the use of implements described in cuts.* In time, indeed, products were increased and this made ever increasing demands for changes in the farmstead.

Though the use of natural power as an aid to work in the barn had been common practice for generations, as described in the first chapters, mechanics for manual aids were late in development. James Meikle designed a winnowing machine around 1720, but Richard

Bradley's *Complete Body of Husbandry*, published in 1727, had no mention of barn machinery in the 1756 edition. A primitive chaff-cutter was introduced as a 'cutting box' about 1760, and in the same year the *Society for the Encouragement of Arts* offered a £20 prize for a machine capable of slicing turnips. In 1770 James Edgill made a spiral knife chaff-cutter and James Sharp advertised a hand mill for splitting beans and grinding malt as well as a winnowing machine that cleaned and sorted grain. That change had come to the farmstead was made clear in James Sharp's book of 1777, *Description of Some of the Utensils of Husbandry: A First Study of Barn Machinery* (Plate 113). This was indeed the first time a comprehensive collection of mechanical farm tools were shown together. Each one made the task of crushing or cutting grain and other fodder easier. They relied on simple mechanics, but they exhibited both technical ingenuity and more directly improved manufacturing processes. The production of tools was increasingly by manufacturers known on a national basis instead of being restricted to the local blacksmith. All these tools were portable. They were used in barns—or within any other type of covered area. They did not need much space and, therefore, they did not have much impact on building layout. Water-driven, and later steam-driven machines always had a capacity for secondary-power take-off points coupled-up by belting to the primary source, but manual tools were less likely to become fixtures.

Many new inventions and patents were introduced from 1770 to the time of Victoria's coronation in 1837. There was a spate of designs for threshing and cutting. In 1774, a trio designed a threshing machine which rubbed out the grain (Smart of Wark, Ilderton of Alnwick, and Oxley of Flodden). A decade later, William Winlaw made another for rubbing, and Andrew Meikle made one to beat out grain. In 1794, James Cooke patented a chaff-cutter with blades on the spokes of a wheel. By the end of the Napoleonic Wars there were many improved slicers, pulpers and mills.

As the nineteenth century progressed, though manual work never ceased altogether on the farm, horse and steam power began to take over (page 152). There were some new developments for manually turned machinery. Early in the century, small hand-machines were introduced to separate grain by revolving beaters. An all-iron hand threshing machine was patented by H. A. Thompson and was illustrated in the Catalogue for the Great Exhibition of 1851. Sheaves were fed into a drum which beat out the corn. It took five men and boys to work it: two to turn the handle, one to place the sheaves, one to handle the grain into sacks, and one to fork away the chaff.

The change to mechanization was not always popular. As new mechanical threshers became available, first in Scotland and later in southern England, especially when powered by water, the farm workers

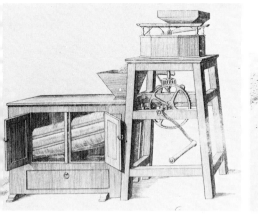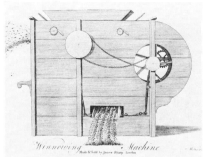

(a) a quernstone mill and rolling mill   (b) the improved winnowing machine of 1770

(c) a hand mill for splitting beans   (d) a chaff-cutter for cattle feed

113. JAMES SHARP AND HIS BARN MACHINERY, 1777

114. THOMPSON'S HAND THRESHING MACHINE
1851

began to see their steady winter work flailing the corn in the barn, hard though it might be, taken from them. During the winter riots of 1830, discontented gangs of labourers destroyed many of these threats to employment on the farms from Devon to York. Little could they have foreseen how far mechanization would eventually oust manual work.

Ox Power

Cave paintings have shown prehistoric draught oxen. The ox has been a beast of burden from early days. A team for oxen was codified in AD 945 within the Welsh Laws of Hywel Dda (also known as Howel Da). A team comprised twelve men—two for plough making, eight to supply the ox and two for the work. The *Domesday Book* of 1086 made the ox central to land measurement. The *caruca* was confirmed as the measure of arable land which could be managed within a year by an eight-ox team, with four being required to serve any one plough. Areas varied due to soil and other local conditions, but 120 acres became a general measure for most of Britain. Horses were sometimes used for ploughing by the Normans but they were inferior in strength. However, as cultivation of arable land increased, the horse slowly began to replace the ox from 1500 to 1750 as the major draught animal. The great cart-horses had the additional value of being more suitable both in war and on the new turnpike roads.

Early breeds of oxen were rough animals in medieval England, generally descendants of the Celtic shorthorn, *Bos longifrons*. Sir Anthony Fitzherbert in his *Boke of Husbandry*, published in 1523, showed a typical pair of oxen which, even allowing for artistic licence, had little similarity to the breed known three centuries later (Plate 115).

115. MEDIEVAL OXEN PLOUGH 1523

During the seventeenth and eighteenth centuries new genetic strains were introduced and prize oxen were highly valued. The engraving by William Ward of the *Newbus Ox* in the mezzotint of 1812 (Plate 116), shows how the yeoman farmer valued his prize beast, specially chopping its root fodder outside its own quarters. In the background is a view of pastoral England at the time of the Napoleonic Wars.

116. *The Newbus Ox*, 1812

The development of new ploughs which suited the horse in the nineteenth century eventually ousted the ox. Finally, oxen were used only for open work for haulage on the wolds and uplands. A few landowners persevered with the ox as a matter of pride and respect for the animal. The very last team was disbanded in 1964 on the Cirencester estate of Lord Bathurst—whose ancestor had founded the Royal College of Agriculture.

Oxen were for haulage and for ploughing. They had no real value as a source of power in the farmstead, though a few cases are recorded. Vittorio Zonca published his *Novo Teatro de Machine et Edifici* in Padua in 1607 which shows a drawing of an inclined treadmill worked by two oxen to work a pair of stones for grinding corn. But this is a rare example and the main influence of oxen on the farmstead lies with their great carts. The development of the ox cart is a study in itself, and it has been well described by Geraint Jenkins in *The English Farm Wagon: Origins and Structure* (David & Charles, 1961). Access for the great corn and hay wagons and tumbrils influenced the layout of yards and of barn doors, and the haulage of tree trunks to the sawmill was a feature of many farmsteads. Oxen had their own stalls and boxes for winter-time which became a particular feature of model farms. But the draught ox was not a mainstay in the development of power in the farmstead.

General References

1. J. S. Creasy, *The Draught Ox*, Institute of Agricultural History, University of Reading, 1974.
2. A. Fenton, 'Draught oxen in Britain', *Bull. d'Ethnographie Tchecoslovaque*, iii–iv, 1969, pp. 17–51.

Donkey Power

The donkey or ass, and more particularly its crossbreed the mule, have had a bad press. Literature has many references to their character, though ass's milk is a well-known luxury for tender skins. Bartholomew Anglicus writing in medieval times on contemporary lore wrote that though the ass was a useful beast of burden and 'is fair of shape and disposition while young and tender ... but the elder he is the fouler he waxeth from day to day ... and he is a melancholy beast'.

Columella, writing his famous books on husbandry in the first century AD (see page 20), recommended that the corn mill should be located near the villa and that the upper stone (the catillus) should be rotated by capstan turned by one or two donkeys—unless as a punishment replaced by slaves. Cato, two centuries previously, had suggested there should be one single-donkey mill for every four persons employed. However, L. A. Moritz, in his *Grain Mills and Flour in Classical Antiquity* (Oxford, 1958), believes this must be too high a ratio since each mill would have ground less than 4.5 kilograms daily.

The donkey has made other contributions in farmstead development. The landscape of parts of Swaledale and Wensleydale is remarkable for its patchwork of fields and outlying barns which are integrated by a management system to cope with the topography of the dales. By the mid-eighteenth century there was a close relation between dairy farming in the dales and sheep rearing on the moors, both worked from nucleated village communities. In the dales the stone-walled fields were small and in places there could be a field barn to every two or three fields, tending to become sparser at the edges of the valleys. Most of the barns were placed at the field boundaries, facing south, irrespective of gradient. Each barn measured about 5 × 10 metres on plan and would hold some four cattle, tethered in pairs, plus additional calf space at one end. The stalls were backed by the access passage and the mew, that is the space for storing hay. The latter was also stored in balks, that is in the loft, which on the hillsides might have access from the higher ground. The milk from dairy farming was used for the distinctive

117. UPPER SWALEDALE, North Yorkshire

cheese of Wensleydale, but commercial cheese production from such a scattered system began to decline in the 1930s and now most of the barns are derelict.[1]

The problem in this kind of farming was to get the small quantities of milk from such outlying shippons. The cows would be milked by hand but it was a long haul back to the village farm for cheese-making. Neither horse nor ox could be economic and, therefore, the donkey came into its own. Donkey power was the basic unit for sustaining the agriculture of the dale. Jimmie the milk donkey was still taking his panniers of milk churns at Castle Bolton in Wensleydale in 1953.

118.
JIMMIE THE MILK DONKEY,
Castle Bolton, Wensleydale
1953

[1] G. Muter, 'The Buildings of Wensleydale—A Study in Local Vernacular Design', Thyssen Research Thesis, 1974.

119.
DONKEY WHEEL
1900

120. DOG WHEEL. 19th century

The donkey also was used on the treadwheel. This was rare compared with the use of the horse-driven horizontal wheels, but the donkey still worked the wheel at Annables Farm, Kinsbourne Green, Hertfordshire in 1900 (Plate 119). Power generated by a donkey was comparatively light. It was used mainly for lifting buckets of liquid or feed. As an alternative to the donkey, the dog could be used. The dog-cart has been a feature in some towns and dogs have been used in America on treadmills for crushing apples and in Wales on wheels for churning milk. A nineteenth-century dog-wheel is on show at the Welsh National

Folk Museum which was taken from Dolellog, Rhostryfan, Caernarvon-
shire (Plate 120). The inclined plane of the treadwheel, against which
the dog must walk or hang, has a simple mechanism for making butter.
Usually, there would be two dogs.

General References

1. H. Brunner, 'Donkey Wheels as a Source of Power', *Country Life*, 28
   December 1972, pp. 1770–1.
2. J. K. Major, *Animal-Powered Machines*, Batsford, 1978.

Horse Power

From ancient times, men have used the horse both for riding and as a
source of power. Power could be direct, as in haulage, or indirect via the
horse mill or wheel. The concept of 'horse power' was defined by James
Watt when he tried to measure mechanical power from steam engines.
The horse, then being replaced, became the standard measure. Watt
experimented with horses that operated the pit cages of the new coal
mines. He found that a horse could pull 150 pounds (68 kilograms)
suspended from a pulley and within one minute raise it 220 feet (67
metres). One horse power required to lift this weight was equal to
$150 \times 220 \times 32$ foot poundals per minute. With the end of imperial
measures the romantic standard of the horse power will fade into
history books. But, since it is equivalent to some 745 watts, the name of
its originator will live on.

The great horse of legend, which was the descendant of the English
black horse, had three variations bred for the dray, the wagon and the
cavalry. In late medieval times, these began to replace oxen on the farm
(page 126). Eventually, their descendants became the famous and distinctive shire-horses. The equally famous Suffolk punch dates from
1506, being later recorded in Camden's *Britannia* of 1586.

Horse power, in remote communities, was an important matter. Major
projects would be undertaken collectively by the village and surrounding farms. The churchyard at Hoxne in Suffolk was extended in 1906
and this required a new approach-track for which gravel had to be
carted. The community mustered about thirty horse power, together
with some eighteen carts, for the project, as revealed at the lunch break
(Plate 121).

Horses were used sometimes instead of donkeys to raise water. This
was a practice which continued until steam power proved to be more
effective. In 1734, 'a new engine for raising water in which horses or
other animals draw without any loss of power' was demonstrated by
Walter Churchman to the Royal Society (Plate 122). It was an elaborate
treadmill and it was unlikely to have been adopted.[1] Simple horse mills

[1] H. Brunner and J. K. Major, 'Water Raising by Animal Power', *Journal of the
History of Industry and Technology*, Vol. 9, No. 2, 1972, pp. 117–51.

121. COMMUNITY HORSE POWER, Hoxne, Suffolk. 1906

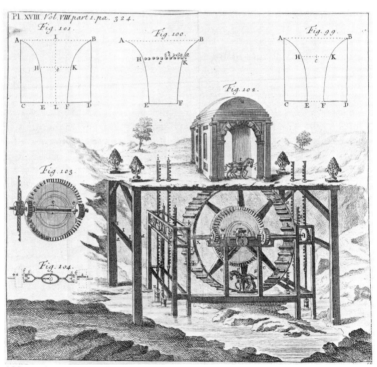

122. WALTER CHURCHMAN'S HORSE ENGINE. 1734

were known in the seventeenth century. One was illustrated by Böckler in 1661 in his *Theatrum Machinarum Novum*. The main development of the use of horses for power on the farm came in the late eighteenth century and, to some extent, began to compensate for the drift of labour into the industrial towns. A horse-driven wheel to turn a butter churn was installed, probably before 1800, at Broughton in Buckinghamshire.

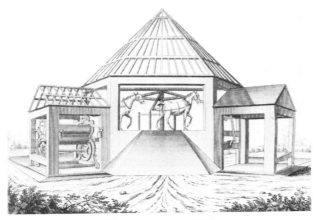

123. SUGAR MILL. 1799

Arthur Young in his sixth volume of his *Annals of Agriculture*, published in 1799, illustrated a horse-driven grinding mill within an hexagonal building (shown unclad) (Plate 123). The three horses are harnessed to a pillar at the centre of a raised platform. As it turns, it operates three levers under the floor that are linked to the three mills where revolving cylinders grind the sugar canes of the Southern States of America. The mills are in structures attached to the hexagon and carts can unload their crops into them direct.

A portable threshing machine, operated by horses, was exhibited in about 1800 at the Woburn Agricultural Meeting, but by the mid-century steam was replacing horse threshers until, in 1867, the judges at the Royal Show ruled that there should be no more prizes given for horse-drawn threshing machines. However, horse-powered field machinery evolved throughout the century and Savage's famous catalogue shows a wide range of cutters, rakes and binders. A simple portable horse-wheel could operate an elevator to assist rick-making. Horse-worked cutter-bars (Plate 125) did not change fundamentally until the tractor ended the use of horse power.

The idea of having fixed horse-gearing at the barn which could operate overhead-line shafting, via a series of pulleys and belts, and work barn machinery on the first floor was developed by T. W. Wedlake in Essex and marketed before 1850. The firm started a foundry in 1809,

124.   HORSE-POWERED FIELD TOOLS AND ELEVATOR

125. EDWARDIAN CUTTER-BAR in transit

having been corn merchants since 1784 at Hornchurch. They were typical of the emergent agricultural engineers. Their horse-wheel was closely integrated with the barn structure and one horse could mill beans, bruise oats, cut chaff or slice turnips. A fixed spindle turned a cast-iron shaft from which a drive was taken over the horse to turn a wooden crown-wheel with cast-iron teeth. The principle was always to have wood and metal engaging each other in such mechanisms.

Most horse-wheels were covered as single-storey buildings outside the main barn. They could be round, square or polygonal in plan, supporting conical or pyramidal roofs. Many were built throughout the nineteenth century.[2, 3] The wheelhouse was a distinctive farm building. In the north it was often called a gin-gan, and in Angus a mill-ging. Generally, it was sited on the north side of the farm and adjacent to the stack yard and threshing barn. The wheelhouse was built to cover an 'overshot' wheel or, sometimes at a later stage, an 'undershoot' wheel, or even portable threshing equipment, although the latter would be expensive. Though some were operated by one horse, most used teams of four to six horses and even, in Scotland, a double team of six horses.[4]

The principles of the horse-wheel are shown in the diagram (Plate 129) from J. C. Morton's *A Cyclopaedia of Agriculture*, published in 1855, though early threshing machines had become general in northern parts before 1800. *The General View of the Agriculture of the County of Northumberland*, written in 1797 by J. Bailey and G. Culley, had noted

[2] J. A. Hellen, 'Agricultural Innovation and Detectable Landscape Margins—The Case of Wheelhouses in Northumberland', *Agriculture History Review*, Vol. 20, 1972, Pt. II, pp. 140–54.

[3] J. A. Hellen, 'Agrarian History Unobserved—19th Century Wheelhouses', *Country Life*, 11 November 1971, pp. 1325–6.

[4] A. J. Riley, 'When Horses Turned the Mill—Some Scottish Survivals', *Country Life*, 27 November 1969, pp. 1415–16.

126. CONICAL WHEELHOUSE, Bitchfield, Belsay Castle, Northumberland, with stone piers and slate roof

127. APSIDAL WHEELHOUSE, West Moorhouses Farm, Matfen Hall, Northumberland, with stone piers

128. POLYGON WHEELHOUSE, High Horton Farm, Blyth, Northumberland, with stone piers and pantile roof

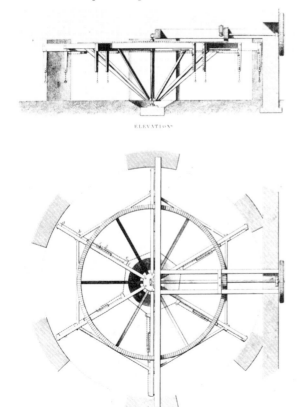

ELEVATION

129. OVERHEAD WHEEL, for six horses, Scotland. 1855

130. WHEELHOUSE, Penpillick, St. Blazey, Cornwall

this and had observed: 'They are all upon the principle of the flax mill, which principle was first introduced into this county for threshing corn near 20 years since by Mr Gregson of Wark.' A machine of small dimensions at that time could be erected for £50 which, with two horses, could thresh and dress 120 bushels of oats or 60 of wheat in eight hours. Since flail threshing might yield 7 bushels per day for a cost of 4d to 6d, horse-wheels quickly became popular. Loudon, in his *Encyclopædia* of 1833, stated that threshing machines were justified when the tillage land required two or more ploughs. However, they were being replaced by steam power so that by the 1840s horse wheelhouses were only common on the smaller farm where they had a long life. In the fifth edition in 1908 of Stephen's *Book of the Farm* there were still three plates showing the design of horse-wheels.

The designs varied, but the overall diameter of the heavy wheel could be up to 8 metres and 2.5 metres off the ground, being supported on a centre post set between a base plate and the plummer block. Thus, the largest wheelhouse would normally measure 9 metres × 4.5 metres high.

Horses were harnessed by yoke-bars to horizontal and radial horse-beams and moved anticlockwise. The crown-wheel, from which a pinion operated, transferred the drive power along a tumbling shaft to the threshing machine in the adjacent barn. A standard four-horse wheel operated at 3 rpm, equal to a speed of 2¼ mph. A good horse exerted up to 77 kilograms on to his yoke-bar but it was essential for the pivot to be properly balanced.

Only a few complete examples of machinery remain. The example at Penpillick (Plate 130) shows the main pivotal shaft and wheel with the massive overhead collar-beam. J. A. Hellen has recorded that in Northumberland in 1970 there were 184 round and 92 polygon wheel-houses still intact but none had an intact wheel. Moreover, another 299 had been completely demolished. They are rapidly disappearing as a feature of corn farmland.

General references

1. J. G. Jenkins, *The English Farm Wagon*, David & Charles, 1961 and 1972.
2. J. K. Manor, *Animal-Powered Engines*, Batsford, 1978.
3. P. A. Wright, *Salute the Carthorse*, Ian Allan, 1971.

3 Indirect Power Sources

Fuel sources for cooking and for warmth have been one of man's great preoccupations. They have their own legends. We remember St. Wenceslas mainly in relation to his task of collecting fuel. The use of warm air, derived from a furnace, to dry fodder or to cure flesh has been practised for more than two millennia. This is an elementary example of the use of indirect power in the service of agriculture. It predates the Industrial Revolution when indirect power changed civilization and agriculture with it.

The harnessing of steam is seen as the immediate result of the new scientific enquiry of the eighteenth century though its real benefits did not materialize in agriculture until after the Napoleonic Wars. Field-work by remote-controlled ploughs (Plate 142) and barns with their attached, tall chimneys (Plate 145) brought to agriculture part of the factory image. Agriculture is an industry. As such, its real exploitation came not via steam but, later, by diesel and electricity. Gas had a short heyday before diesel power was introduced and is now associated mainly with specialized tasks, using container gas rather than piped gas.

The combustion engine and the generator or fusebox are the mainstay of modern, industrialized agriculture. They have changed our concepts of what a farmstead is from a series of barns and byres, grouped to shelter each other, to a series of factory sheds. Thus, in the two examples illustrated in Plates 131 and 132 there can be seen the real distinction between the traditional and the modern farm. This is what the Industrial Revolution means in terms of farm building. The traditional farm had the house, livestock and implements integrated under one roof. The modern farm has a layout for the efficient handling of materials divorced from the farm dwelling.

Farm wastes have always been considered both as a nuisance and as an important by-product. Grain leaves a straw waste which may be valuable for livestock bedding, for thatch or, today, for cellulose extracts. Livestock, inevitably, produce effluent. Mixed with bedding, this can produce farmyard manure (FYM). The dunghill or midden is an important feature of traditional, mixed farms. Lucius Columella (page 20) gave sound advice in the first century AD, 'Let there be also two dunghills, one of which may receive new off-scourings and filth, and

131. FARMSTEAD at Muhen, Switzerland

132. CONTROLLED ENVIRONMENT POULTRY HOUSES, England

keep them a whole year; and a second, from which the old may be carried. But let both of them have their bottoms somewhat shelving, with a gentle descent, in the manner of ponds, both well built and paved, that they may not let the moisture pass through; for it is of great importance, that the dung retain its strength by the juice of it not being dried up ...' The fertilizer value of effluent depends on it not leaking away. Today, however, a major change has taken place. Processing effluent can yield an indirect power source as discussed in the section on gas power. The concept of *total energy* (see page 204) may also change the future farmstead as much as has the materials-handling revolution of the last few decades.

Warm Air and Solid Fuel

Corn needs to be dry if it is to be kept before it is ground to make meal. Ideally, if it is not to become mildewed or fermented, it needs to have a moisture content of under 14 per cent to last through the long winter months. To last indefinitely, it needs to be under 10 per cent. The Egyptians had no trouble since their corn was dry when harvested. Joseph, as Genesis states, collected the harvest during the seven plenteous years in the land of Egypt and laid it up in the cities, gathering 'corn as the sand of the sea, very much until he left numbering; for it was without number'. During the following seven years of dearth, there was bread throughout the land of Egypt even though there was famine over the face of all the rest of the earth. Storing grain in such bulk for so long a period must have posed a major management problem. Not much is known about the storage methods. However, some tomb paintings do show the great grain bunkers; the design changed very little throughout ancient Egyptian civilization and it was continued in the Graeco-Roman period. The earliest recorded example was in a tomb of the First Dynasty at Saqqara (Plate 133).[1] The beehive-type structures were of adobe, the sun-baked mud bricks of Egypt, simply vaulted, and with an opening in the top for filling. The larger vaults had stairs to reach the top.

In warm climates, grain can be stored for long periods in well-ventilated containers. The corn is dry, though not as sun baked as in Egypt, and a warm breeze is all that is needed to keep it in condition. Specialist buildings are to be found in many parts of the world. The distinctive horreos of Galicia (Plate 134), in north-west Spain, are a feature of the vernacular granaries of the region, being ventilated by Atlantic breezes through their slats and with staddle stones to keep the rats from entry (see Plate 55).

[1] Gua tomb: report from A. J. Spencer, Department of Egyptian Antiquities, British Museum.

133.
GRANARIES ON
WOODEN COFFIN,
Gua, Saqqara
1st Dynasty

134. GRANARIES, Galicia, Spain

Keeping corn in cold, wet, northern countries was never simple. Iron Age Celts built racks high above their stone-hearthed fires, on which they laid their eared straw prior to threshing. In Iona, one drying kiln was large enough for the straw to be threshed adjacent to the racked area. The Welsh Laws of Hywel Dda (page 126) referred to the king's piped kiln which could also be used to lodge his huntsmen. Kilns, obviously, were important places.

Hot-air ducts were introduced by the Romans who, being expert in such domestic luxuries, had begun to use the method for corn drying before they left their northern province. A fourth-century Roman corn-drying kiln, adjacent to the River Lea near Hertford, was excavated in 1975 and then removed and rebuilt at Hertford Museum (Plate 135).[2] A fire at the stoke hole circulated hot air through the flue to the central plenum chamber. Above the chamber, the floor would have been of split boards coated with clay to keep the grain from falling through the gaps. In more sophisticated kilns, perforated Roman tiles would have been used—a practice still used in this century, especially for drying malt barley. The plenum walls were made of chalk blocks, flint and stone, bonded in a mixture of cement, crushed chalk and clay which permitted considerable thermal movement without cracking. The drying area measured some 3 × 3 metres. Chaff and waste straw, after the straw had been flailed, would have been used to fuel the furnace to dry further batches of corn.

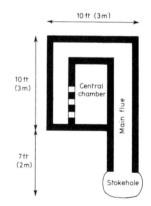

135. ROMAN CORN DRIER, Hertford, plan and view
     4th century

[2] Hertford corn drier: report from C. Partridge, Eastern Region Archaeological Services, Hertford.

136. MEDIEVAL FARMSTEAD, Sadler's Wood, Lewknor, Oxfordshire, looking north. The east end of the steading, the purpose of which is obscure, showing the north–south drain which took water from the yard to an external ditch. The rooms were domestic to the west (off picture) but these semi-service rooms and the entrance have not been clearly identified. The building was over 25 metres long of which about 8 metres is shown, being single storied, of tiled roof and timber frame with wattle-and-daub panels. To the east of the photograph are the remains of other structures, which might have predated or been contemporary with the house and which measured 11 × 4.5 metres. At the eastern end of this range was what seems to have been a corn-drying unit. It had mortared roofing tiles laid flat over a U-shaped room

Corn drying remained a feature of life in medieval farmsteads. An abandoned farmstead, which was inhabited and altered several times between about the mid-thirteenth century up to about AD 1350–1400, was excavated in 1972 during the construction of the M40 motorway near Lewknor on the south-western slopes of the Chilterns escarpment. Previously, this site had been unknown. The quality of the buildings, and of two other medieval sites nearby, is above average for the period. Abingdon Abbey owned most of Lewknor and, therefore, may have been landlords of these farms.[3]

[3] 'Sadler's Wood Farmstead, Lewknor', report by R. A. Chambers, Oxoniensia, Vol. 38, 1973.

137. CORN-DRYING KILN, Patterdale, Cumbria. c. 1600

A different type of corn-drying kiln exists at Patterdale (Plate 137). It is dated circa AD 1600, set on the hillside with an upper entrance to a drying chamber, via a low doorway, with its floor level marked by projecting stone slates above a hearth set between low walls at the lower gradient. Small flues let out excess moisture.

Warm air, fuelled from timber or chaff, rarely from coal, has been used for corn drying over the centuries. In addition, the Great Stoves, the forerunners and later the aids of glasshouses, often circulated warm air to assist forced fruits and vegetables (page 86). The practice was replaced by steam power and, later, by other fossil fuels and electricity. But, in one form or another, warm air remains an essential feature of crop husbandry. It can have other uses. Large modern herds of some 200 cows may produce up to 5000 litres of milk at each milking. At release, milk is near blood heat and this has to be chilled to 10 °C immediately. The extracted heat can be circulated to warm calf pens or the milking parlour.

Steam Power

The idea of a steam turbine was referred to by Hero in about 150 BC. The English Royal Society was founded by Charles II to apply science, amongst other disciplines, to agriculture and mechanics. Steam power was already a subject for discussion. The Marquess of Worcester showed in 1663 how water could be raised by pressure from steam. Later, in 1712, Newcomen invented a steam pump for draining Cornish tin mines. However, the great boost for steam power came from the partnership of Matthew Boulton and James Watt, encouraged by the Lunar Society in the Potteries and in Birmingham, during the last quarter of the eighteenth century. In time their work indirectly revolutionized farming methods and, above all, made a fundamental change in farmstead layouts.

The revolution in tillage methods began early in the eighteenth century, half a century after the creation of the Royal Society, with Jethro Tull's new seed-drill. By the time James Watt began to understand the latent power of steam, Tull's two main farming principles had been adopted in most prosperous farming areas. Seed was drilled in regular rows, rather than broadcast, and the land was hoed, that is tilled, after ploughing. At the same time, the plough itself was being radically changed. Arbuthnot introduced his shaped, mould-board plough in 1771 at Ravensbury in Surrey. The height of the blade could be adjusted to suit the horse. The shire-horse then came into its own on English farms.

Steam power was applied on the farm first for threshing, later for ploughing. Experiments took place in Scotland, Northumberland and the West Country, but the first to achieve success was Andrew Meikle in 1786. Meikle was a miller in East Lothian. He developed a drum covered with pegs which revolved over the straw inside a larger drum so that the grain fell out into a bin and the straw was moved away by rollers. Modern threshing machines use the same principle. The use of steam power to turn the drum was the beginning of the new, fossil-fuel powered agriculture. John Wilkinson, the iron-master of Coalbrookdale, installed steam threshing in 1798 on his Denbighshire farm. The rapid growth in the use of the thresher became an urgent matter at the outbreak of the Napoleonic Wars. As farm labourers were press-ganged into Nelson's men-of-war, so mechanization of food production became essential. The pressure of war has been a recurring factor in the development of farm machinery in the nineteenth and twentieth centuries. At the same time, population growth and expanding towns created additional demand for food production.

William Marshall wrote of the thresher in 1804 in his account of *Landed Property*: 'This may be considered as the most valuable discov-

138. (*opposite*) MILKING PARLOUR, Rushbrooke Farm, Thorpe Morieux, Suffolk, for Strutt and Parker Farms. Architect, John B. Weller. The parlour is heated by heat extracted from milk when it reaches the dairy. A low-level grille just shows bottom right. 1971

ery, in machines of agriculture, which has been made for centuries past. Not merely as lessening human labour, but as relieving farm workmen from their most unhealthy employment.' Grain and straw dust, together with damp hay, are potential killers causing 'farmer's lung'.

Arthur Young became one of the growing band of bureaucrats who served agriculture by inspecting it as Secretary for the Board of Agriculture set up in 1793. This forerunner of the Ministry of Agriculture was created to examine productivity in food production. Young rode round the counties of England. He saw how the new revolution in technology was changing the farmstead. He rode through the corn belt of Essex in 1807 and then sent to the Board his *General View of the Agriculture of Essex*. He reported that the mechanical thresher 'promised speedily to put an end to all barn building'. So it has proved to be. Barns to hold unthreshed corn—including the great tithe barns—were the first amongst farm buildings to become redundant, and rural England no longer needed one of its main landscape features.

In 1809, Arthur Young rode through Oxfordshire and reported another *General View* of a county's farming practice. Within two years he had now begun to see that the farmstead needed to be planned to suit mechanization—a matter to which Loudon was soon to apply his mind (page 111). Young reported: 'The position of the threshing mill decides that of every other building, for it cuts or ought to cut all the hay of the farm into chaff, with much of the straw; and the house which immediately receives the chaff must be so placed as to admit a convenient delivery to the stables, stalls and sheepyards. Thus the strawhouse, chaffhouse, stables, stalls, haystacks and sheepyard must be placed in consequence of the position of the threshing-mill or waste and expense of labour must follow.' The point was taken further by William Gooch who was the surveyor for Cambridgeshire. In 1811 he reported on mechanization whereby the corn stacks were moved to the thresher by

139. DEANE, DRAY & DEANE'S STEAM ENGINE AND THRESHER UNIT, as advertised in the Catalogue for the Great Exhibition, 1851

wheeled frames set on iron rails. This was developed further in later years (page 74).

Change within the farmstead can be slow and many prophets are impatient men. Old barns were put to new uses for generations to come. The steam-power unit would stand outside the medieval barn driving a belt which turned the drum of the thresher inside the barn. Wily manufacturers showed how farmers did not need expensive new buildings when they bought their machines (Plate 139)—something which still happens today.

But taking the crop to the machine was not as efficient as the machine to the crop. It was more sensible to take the thresher to corn ricks placed more conveniently in the open. With a steam machine, threshing could be completed within a few dry days in autumn. It did not need the covered space for the long winter of manual work. Copeland in his long review of *Agriculture, Ancient and Modern*, published in 1866, illus-

140. PORTABLE THRESHING MACHINE. 1866

trated how modern practice dispensed with the straw barn (Plate 140). A decade later, most straw was threshed in the field. The evolution of the rick yard as part of the steading, with its effect on layout, was discussed (page 70). The new technology required a team for short periods, not two or four men flailing all winter. This is shown clearly in the photograph of steam threshing at Harlington in Middlesex in 1868

141. THRESHING at Harlington, Middlesex. 1868

(Plate 141). The rick had been formed on a large platform set over staddle stones. This was off-loaded into the thresher and fifteen men were at work including those taking sacked corn into the barn.

Steam power was applied to field work. The earliest steam plough was introduced in 1833 by Heathcoat & Parkes. Later, James Usher in 1844 tried to introduce a new ploughing method, with a rotary action for the blades, so that the power unit and the implement were one machine. It was unsuccessful. Steam ploughs were given a major boost after the Great Exhibition of 1851. By 1868, there were no less than

142. STEAM PLOUGHING TACKLE, Savage's Catalogue (c–d opposite)

143. SAVAGE'S STEAM ENGINE AND TACKLE

fifty-eight 'steam-engines forming an imposing line of funnels, fly-wheels and driving belts' as the *Journal of the Bath and West Society* reported of their annual show. Steam ploughing became a feature of the new, industrial farm landscapes. For the first time, large fields became essential. Savage's catalogue from his King's Lynn factory, shows the new techniques (Plates 142 and 143).

The traditional farm labour-force was inadequate to the new technology. Indeed, not all farmers could afford a steam engine for a few days' work each year. Migrant teams of steam threshers and ploughers, often with their own tackle, became a new feature of the rural community. They disrupted the old order and were an unsettling influence acutely observed by Flora Thompson in *Lark Rise to Candleford*:

> Machinery was just coming into use on the land. Every autumn appeared a pair of large traction engines, which, posted one on each side of a field, drew a plough across and across by means of a cable. These toured the district under their own steam for hire on the different farms, and the outfit included a small caravan, known as 'the box', for the two drivers to live and sleep in. In the 'nineties, when they had decided to emigrate and wanted to learn all that was possible about farming, both Laura's brothers, in turn, did a spell with the steam plough, horrifying the other hamlet people, who looked upon such nomads as social outcasts. Their ideas had not then been extended to include mechanics as a class apart and they were lumped as inferiors with sweeps and tinkers and others whose work made their faces and clothes black....
>
> Such machinery as the farmer owned was horse-drawn and was only in partial use. In some fields a horse-drawn drill would sow the seed in rows, in others a human sower would walk up and down with a basket suspended from his neck and fling the seed with both hands broadcast. In harvest time the mechanical reaper was already a familiar sight, but it only did a small part of the work; men were still mowing with scythes and a few women were still reaping with sickles.

There were always more steam threshing machines than steam ploughs. This was in ratios of between 4:1 and 10:1 in different counties, but the steam engine, whether mobile or fixed, had a place in the farmstead. As a source of power, it had limitations but many new uses were invented for it, including that introduced at Hereford in 1875 by the firm of Newton Wilson. They put on sale a 'Patent Horse and Cattle Groomer' which used steam power, via universal joints, to operate a series of revolving brushes whereby 'the horses cleaned by this machine seem to enjoy the operation'. However, steam was seen as the focal power unit for livestock farming at the beginning of the nineteenth century. Richard Lugar published *The Country Gentleman's Architect* in 1807 and this had a profound influence on rural building a generation before Loudon's *Encyclopædia*. Lugar showed how livestock buildings should be set out radially around the steam boiler (Plate 144). This was one of the earliest attempts to group farm buildings in a circle focused on one operation. The steaming room, with its copper and chimney, was placed centrally. Over the copper was a barrel which contained potatoes. Around the edge of the steam room were troughs acting as cisterns for water or milk and convenient for mixing up the pig meal. The troughs were of brick construction or were covered with Bayley's patent composition or with lead (the effect of lead poisoning being unrecognized). A granary over the steaming room could chute meal into the mixing area. Around the inner building was a lean-to

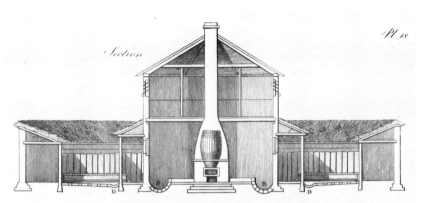

Pl. 18

Section

Plan of a Piggery with steaming Room & Granary over.

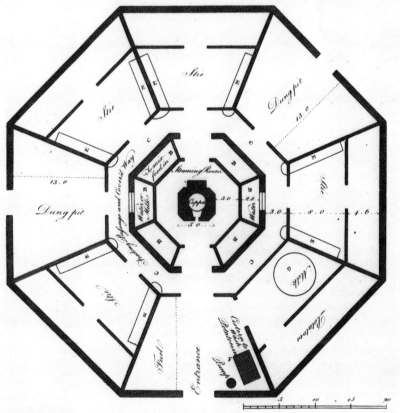

London, Published Sept.r 1 1806 by J. Taylor, 59 High Holborn.

144. LUGAR'S STEAM PIGGERY
1807

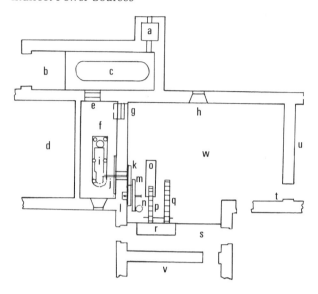

Arrangement on the ground floor with the corn
barn

(a) Chimney-stack, six feet square, fifty feet high
(b) Coal-store, twenty-five feet by five
(c) Boiler-house, twenty-five feet by nine
(d) Stair to granary
(e) Steps to boiler and furnace-house
(f) Engine-house
(g) Door from corn-barn to engine-house
(h) Window in corn-barn
(i) Steam-engine
(j) Main shaft carrying fly-wheel

(k) Intermediate spur-wheel
(l) Intermediate spur-wheel
(m) Great spur-wheel
(n) Hummeller
(o) Second fanner supplied by the elevator (p)
(p) Elevator from first spout
(q) Elevator from second spout
(r) First fanner
(s) Chaff-house
(t) Stair to granary (u)
(u) Granary
(v) Straw-barn
(w) Corn-barn

145. STEAM POWER TO CORN BARN. 1871

work passage from which the open pig yards, with their feed troughs,
could be reached. The four sties had perimeter, monopitch sleeping
areas for the pigs. The other four facets of the octagon were taken up by
two dung pits, convenient to the four sties for forking out bedding, and a
storage area for potatoes and milk for the steamer, and the entrance to
the store for the fuel for the steamer and a pump for the water supply. In
all, it was a positive design for specific management of livestock.

The development of steam led to specialized layouts. *The Book of the
Farm* was published in 1871. It recorded that 'every day as the management of the steam-engine is more and more understood, it is becoming
more in use on farms'. It showed how the steam engine could be
installed adjacent to the barn and preparation rooms and how gearing
and shafts could drive different machinery (Plate 145). The straw
barn (v) was at the furthest point from the great chimney (a) which was
about 2 metres square and 15 metres high. Such chimneys were to

become a feature of many farms. L. H. Ruegg in 1854 wrote about *Farming of Dorsetshire* in the *Journal of the Royal Agricultural Society of England*. He considered that a modern farm which had a tall chimney gave 'activity and animation to a somewhat desolate district'. There was little doubt for the mid-Victorians that the progressive farmer had more to do with industry than with a romantic, pastoral landscape. It introduced the first conflict of identity to the steadings which still remains incompletely resolved.

Steam was not seen as an unmitigated blessing. An explosion at Rockmoor House Farm, Alnwick, Northumberland killed ten people when a 3-ton boiler for a condensing steam engine failed. A report of the incident in *The Builder* of November 1862 advised caution about steam boilers in farmsteads: '... it becomes the duty of farm labourers, totally unacquainted with the properties of steam, to work them, and we have for a result disasters that militate against the use of the new national servant'.

Loudon, of course, considered that the farmstead did not have to be a factory composed of characterless buildings. They could reflect 'civilized' architectural values, whether Gothic or Classical did not matter. He illustrated a model farm, with its own main entrance drive and portico, and dominated by the steam-driven mill and Classical chimney shaft and backed up with a symmetrical layout for the stockyards. The latter had style with arcades, archways and pilasters (Plate 146).

The great period of agricultural prosperity was from the time of the Great Exhibition of 1851 up to about 1875. It ended with the import of cheap corn from America and the invention of refrigerated ships for

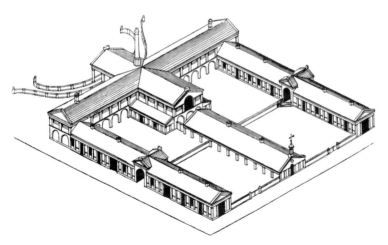

146. LOUDON'S FARM in Grecian style,
    Encyclopædia, 1833

meat. However, during this quarter century steam power was the driving force in the Industrial Revolution and this coincided with the erection of many model farmsteads. The industrial farm chimney became a feature of many arable farms and the steam shaft for boiling pig swill a secondary feature. The Victorians cared for composition. Though few had the Grecian trappings suggested by Loudon, many were symmetrical in design with the chimney given pride of place. On simpler, working farms, the chimney would still be dominant but, as the *Book of the Farm* illustrated, it would be set to one side—particularly when, as normally happened, a medieval or Georgian steading was improved by introducing steam power. A serious limitation of steam engines was that they were best placed close to the fuel bunker and, therefore, the range of materials that could be handled was limited to the practical layout of shafts and belts. The coalhouse, boiler, chimney and engine would be housed adjacent to the work area where straw would be threshed, chaff cut and corn rolled. The livestock feed and bedding still had to be man-handled into the yards.

General references

1. H. Bonnett. *Saga of the Steam Plough*, David & Charles, 1972.
2. D. Braithwaite, *Savage of King's Lynn*, Patrick Stevens, Cambridge, 1975.
3. N. E. Fox, 'The Spread of the Threshing Machine in Central Southern England'; and S. Macdonald, 'Further Progress with the Early Threshing Machine—a Rejoinder', *Agricultural History Review*, Vol. 26, Pt. 1, 1978, pp. 26–32.
4. S. Macdonald, 'The Progress of the Early Threshing Machine', *Agricultural History Review*, Vol. 23, Pt. 1, 1975, pp. 63–77.
5. R. Trow-Smith, *Power on the Land*, Agripress, 1975.
6. P. Wright, *Traction Engines*, A. & C. Black.

Gas Power

Farms, like other premises, have been lit by town gas when this has been available. For a brief period, gas-powered engines were used during the 1880s and were shown at the Royal Show in 1888. However, before they could challenge steam as a primary source for power, both were superseded by the evolution of the internal combustion engine.

The development of mass housing for broiler chickens during the late 1940s created specific requirements for well-insulated and environmentally controlled buildings. Compressed and liquified gas proved an economic fuel. Since the heat source was self-contained, it meant that buildings could be grouped together on remote sites, which was important for disease control. Propane and butane gas, by-products

148. (opposite) SUSPENDED HEATERS FOR CHICKS

147. LIQUIFIED GAS CYLINDERS AND BROILERS
    1950s

of the coal industry, became a familiar part of intensive poultry husbandry. A stressed-skin, plywood-panelled broiler house was developed in the late 1950s by the Plywood Manufacturers Association of British Columbia (Plate 147). It shows typical gas cylinders with their pressure valve outside the building and correctly installed on a concrete base. The spherical, white cylinders of some companies became a distinctive feature in the countryside. Inside, day-old chicks are reared for only twelve weeks. The suspended heaters are raised above the first brood-

ing areas until groups are held in big circular arenas. The hardboard pens are removed during the last stages of the fattening process and the broilers then use the whole floor.

Methane gas as a power source, derived from animal wastes, remains the great hope of many pioneers. As early as 1806, Humphrey Davy, famous for his experiments involving mine gases, recorded that animal waste gave off methane gas. Methane gas lighting was provided from livestock effluents on several farms in Germany during the 1890s and on a few in Britain before the First World War. Several plants were installed during the Second World War. But quantities produced were not equal to the power required for driving machinery.

The first serious attempt to use methane as a power source was made by L. J. Fry on his farm eight miles from Johannesburg in 1957.[1] He collected all the effluent from 900 pigs into a digester, where it became anaerobic and, as a by-product, released methane which is a hydrocarbon (CH_4) of about 70 per cent methane and 30 per cent carbon dioxide. The methane was collected in a holder under its own pressure and was used to power a converted Crossley HD3 diesel engine which was most suited to work with the gas of 120 octane rating. Waste heat was used to maintain the temperature in the digester. The digester not only produced 150 cubic metres of methane each day but, as a byproduct, a good friable fertilizer. The engine was able to work continuously to provide 10 brake horse power, being used to pump boreholes, spray irrigation, dry grass, heat water, and for other equipment and lighting around the farm. It could be used to dry the fertilizer for bagging and sale.

With larger livestock units, producing considerable effluent, the production of methane is an attractive idea. Wright Rain Ltd. decided to develop a prototype, package-deal unit which was demonstrated in 1963 and aimed to suit units of 800 pigs or 130 cows (Plate 149).

The methane plant did not go into production. The main problem in northern countries is that all the heat available from the methane produced is required during the winter months to keep the digester at the required temperature of 18 to 38 °C. Indeed, in severe weather, additional heat input is required. The main developments in the use of digesters during the 1970s have been at Craibstone experimental farm near Aberdeen conducted by the Scottish Farm Buildings Investigation Unit (Plate 150). Even with 50-millimetre insulation, the gas released from 450 litres of effluent each day was inadequate to provide useful power all the year round.

Some patent systems were marketed in the mid-1970s, such as the Bio-gas Methane Plant. The digester tank was of butyl rubber within a 75-millimetre glass-fibre blanket. The methane was produced via a heat

[1] L. J. Fry, *Practical Building of Methane Power Plants for Rural Energy Independence*, D. A. Knox, Andover, 1974.

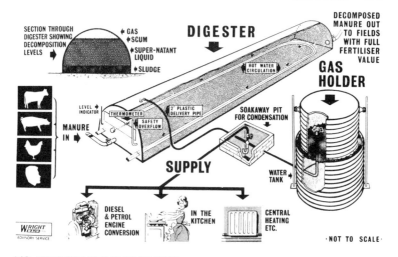

149. WRIGHT RAIN METHANE UNIT
1963

150. CRAIBSTONE EXPERIMENTAL DIGESTER, view of gas holder, digester
boiler house and sundry tanks
1974

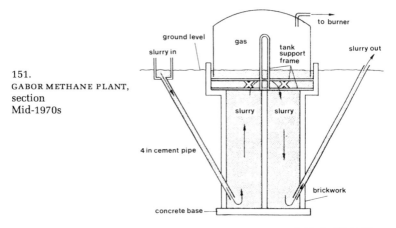

151.
GABOR METHANE PLANT,
section
Mid-1970s

152. METHANE UNIT, Bore Place, Chiddingstone, Kent. Late 1970s

exchanger for a hot water system. The Intermediate Technology Development Group have made some studies of the systems required for methane. The main developments have been in warm countries. The Indian Government has promoted methane plants for use in Bombay District which can be constructed mainly from local bricks and concrete, with a small kit of metal components. These have been supervised by the Khadi Village Industry Commission since 1960. Each cow can produce 10 kilograms of effluent a day which can provide 0.35 cubic metres of methane and this is enough to provide cooking facilities for one person.

In the last years of the 1970s, several developments in methane production took place. The unit, shown in Plate 152, designed by Helix of Reading, stores effluent from 320 cows underground where it is digested to produce methane which, in turn, generates electricity with an output of 25 kilowatts plus 33 kilowatts of heat. This is used to power the lighting, heating, milking and mill-mixing for the entire dairy unit. The digester tanks are covered by floating, fibreglass, troughed lids weighted down by concrete blocks. The pump house is adjacent, and set back are the cow kennels. Elm-boarded walls were a by-product from the Dutch elm disease on the farm.

General reference

C. Bell, S. Boulter, D. Dunlop and P. Keiller, *Methane—the Fuel of the Future*, Andrew Singer, Cambridge, 1974

Diesel Power

Steam power, as the main prime mover on the farm, was superseded by the development of the internal combustion engine. The vast wheat lands of Northern America provided the incentive for a new technology. The Charter Engine Co. of Chicago in 1889 converted a Rumley steam tractor to take a gasoline engine for use on the Dakota prairie. Many other tractors were developed within a few years. One of the first designed from first principles was that of John Froelich in Iowa in 1892, though it was of poor performance (Plate 153).

153. FROELICH'S PIONEER TRACTOR
1892

In the United Kingdom, Dan Albone of Biggleswade started to make his twin-engine, 24-horse-power Ivel Agricultural Tractor in 1902. It was one of the first to have a power-take-off (PTO) drive with a pulley to give secondary power to ploughs, threshers or barn machinery. It was this concept, of a mobile source of secondary power, that was to change the design of farmsteads. S. Henderson, writing his *The Modern Farmstead* in 1902 confirmed that the oil engine was 'rapidly taking the place of the steam engine as the motive power in the homestead'.

Sanderson & Marshall began to make tractors. By the outbreak of war in 1914, though few tractors were sold in the UK, the firm had become the largest exporters for tractors in the world. However, this industry was closed down by the urgent need to make guns. In the meantime, Henry Ford had adapted his T-Ford car in 1908 to form the basis for his tractors, later to be of international fame. By 1915, there were thirty United States companies making tractors. UK agriculture was desperate for power as the war progressed. The government imported 6000 Fordson tractors in 1917 in order to help food production.

Contemporary with the evolution of tractor power was the development of the stationary diesel engine for the farmstead. Machine milking, after early attempts at hand pumps, was one of the first tasks to be mechanized. The aim was to get a machine to create alternate suction and pressure to simulate suckling. One of the first was the Thistle Mechanical Milking Machine which was exhibited in 1895 at the Royal Show and which was patented by Dr. Alexander Shields of Glasgow (Plate 154). It had some disadvantages. The pulsator had to be near its diesel engine and, being connected by tubing, it lost efficiency. It therefore required a large air pump, and this created a noise that could be heard two miles away. In addition, contamination of milk was a serious problem. Though many were installed, the firm became defunct

154. THISTLE MECHANICAL MILKING MACHINE
1895

in 1898. A better machine was marketed in 1915 by the Associated Manufacturers' Company. It was known as the Amanco and was claimed to milk twenty-five cows in an hour—as against eight to twelve by hand milking (Plate 155). It was a major improvement on the Neilson Milking Machine of 1892 (page 121).

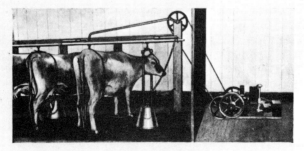
155. AMANCO MILKER
1915

The stationary engine continued to be developed throughout the inter-war years. Static engines in 1908 provided farmers collectively with 46,000 horse power, which had become 108,000 horse power by 1913 and 540,000 by 1939. By 1950, there were some 200,000 engines on UK farms. Their study has become a matter of research (pioneered by David Edginton), recorded in the 1970s in the journal *The Stationary Engine Advertiser* which illustrated four examples all of which had a revolutionary impact on the farmstead (Plates 156 to 159).

156. WOLSELEY PORTABLE PETROL ENGINE

Some machines required a more refined fuel than diesel. It was a major change in the farmstead to have a small, wheeled power-source which could be moved to any ground-floor work position, complete with its own chocks, in order to be coupled up to other equipment with a short belt drive. In Plate 156 the engine is driving a cream separator (see also Plates 111 and 173). But, equally, it could work any other barn machinery such as thresher, crusher, sheller, cleaner or elevator.

Grid electricity was slow in reaching remote farms (see page 171). The small engine which could be coupled to a dynamo to generate power for electric light was to be found on many farms, in some cases still being used today, especially as a stand-by.

By the 1940s, diesel engines had become powerful. They could be used to drive large grain-drying plant, as in the case of the Ruston & Hornsby 17-horse-power engine erected in 1942 (Plate 158). It is now a stand-by engine, in case of power failure, driving a 9.5 kva alternator. Wolseley introduced a new machine (Plate 159) in 1943 via their subsidiary company, the Wolseley Sheep Shearing Machine Co. Ltd. It was introduced in wartime and quickly proved itself adaptable, easy starting, silent and robust.

The period 1919–39 was one of rapid development of the tractor. The

157. (*left*) WOLSELEY DIRECT COUPLED LIGHTING SET

159. (*right*) NEW WOLSELEY FARM ENGINE. 1943

158. RUSTON & HORNSBY 17 HORSE-POWER ENGINE. 1942

Royal Agricultural Society of England tested thirty-six different tractors in 1920 which could drive ploughs, harrows, drills and threshers as well as pull all manner of loads. By 1939, there were 60,000 tractors on UK farms. Horse power was beginning to decline. In 1881, there had been 937,000 farm horses. By 1939, these had dropped to about 660,000, that is eleven for every tractor. However, the latter was already giving two-thirds of all mobile farm power. The combine harvester was developed in 1928, though only 150 were in use on UK farms by 1939. Grain drying, an adjunct of harvesting, began in the same period with a number of experimental techniques. Grass drying, too, began in 1933 but only eighty driers had been installed by 1939.

160. DRIER TRIALS, Roke Farm, Benson, Oxfordshire. 1932

Milk production became more sophisticated. Milk recording was instituted in 1913, but the impetus for change came with the creation of the Milk Marketing Board in 1933. The Board remains one of the most effective nationally based liaisons between producer and consumer in the world. Pipeline milking from the pulsator cluster to the churn cooler in the dairy began in the early 1920s. A. J. Hosier had introduced a wheeled releaser plant in 1922 and portable bails in 1927 (see page 185). In 1926, W. S. Abbot began to batch group his cows, according to yield, to milk them in special stalls on his farm in Northamptonshire.

Mechanization was given a major boost during the war years and following the 1947 Agriculture Act. The 60,000 UK tractors of 1939 became 260,000 by 1949 and 478,000 by 1956. The forearm loader attachment made the tractor a versatile machine in the 1950s, especially with Rex Patterson's invention of the buckrake for handling grass—later being replaced by the forage harvester. A wide range of attachments of bucket, scoop, fork, etc., made every pushing and lifting requirement for farm materials that much easier. By degrees, the turning movement of the tractor and its attachment became one of the main criteria for the layout of many buildings.

Charles Hurford illustrated in 1960 how a grass crop could be completely mechanized from harvesting to consumption by a combination of diesel and electrical power (Plate 161). A cutter-bar harvests the crop and a crimper bruises it and places it in a neat swathe. Ideally, this is left to wilt for twenty-four hours. A second tractor with forage harvester lifts the swathe, chops it and blows it into a rear forage box. The latter has a revolving floor which moves the grass to an auger when the forage box

162. (opposite) FILLING A SILAGE CLAMP
1960

161. THE MECHANIZED GRASS CROP
1960

reaches the steading. The chopped grass drops from the vehicle into a
dump box from which it is blown to the top of the tower silo. The type
shown is hermetically sealed, with breather bags and air vents at the
top, and has a bottom-rotating cutter auger and unloader. Adjacent is a
second tower silo for wet grain, also with bottom unloader. Both unload
to an automatic roller-mill which lifts the mixed fodder of haylage and
concentrate on to an auger feeder, which deposits predetermined
rations at each cow-place along the manger. In less automated layouts,
the tractor and forage box drive on to the top of a clamp in a silo barn and
empty the load, compacting the clamp at the same time (Plate 162).

The development of slatted or perforated floors for almost all classes of livestock developed in the 1950s, but became widespread in the 1960s. It was a Victorian idea (see Plate 75). When straw for bedding was expensive, restricted or zero bedding became desirable. This, in turn, created the need to store, handle and deposit liquid effluents or slurry. The vacuum tanker became another PTO attachment for the tractor, sucking effluents from the storage pit, compound or cellar (Plates 163 and 164).

In the early 1970s, the use of tractor cabs with safety frames became required practice. This, in turn, made headroom around the farmstead a much more critical factor if a tractor was to be used both there and in the field.

163, 164 VACUUM TANKER removing and spreading slurry
         1964

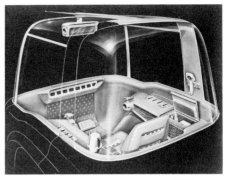

165, 166 EXPERIMENTAL TRACTOR DESIGN and EXPERIMENTAL TRACTOR CAB. 1970

The tractor evolved as a diesel-powered vehicle and other imple-ments have been related to its potential as a power source. It is acknowl-edged to be both inefficient in terms of power utilization and also uncomfortable to operate. Much of its powered-use happens behind the driver. With cabs, noise is considerable and ear-muffs are now essential. Previously many drivers had developed spinal and hearing defects. The Ford Motor Company examined the possibility for a new type of tractor and a scale model was made in about 1970 (Plate 165). A radical change would be for the tractor to work by a power linkage in front of the vehicle for all operations. However, there have also been other experi-ments to produce a robot tractor worked by below-ground guide-cables and sensors on the vehicle or by radar control from a field monitor. It seems almost certain that power mechanics both for field and steading are due for major changes within a generation.

Electrical Power

Electricity transformed the basis of farmstead design, as for all building. In 1908, Beauchamp and Winder published their *Handbook of Farm Buildings* and declared that farm tasks should be powered by electric-ity. They were prophets ahead of their age. The electrical revolution on the farm was not in full swing until half a century later.

The new age was launched by the Electricity (Supply) Acts of 1919 and 1926. The latter introduced the National Grid distribution across the countryside—from town to town. There were probably only ten to twenty farms with an electrical supply. Propaganda to promote farm demand for electricity began in 1928. The British Electrical Develop-ment Association produced a *Practical Cinematograph Film* on *Rural Electrification: showing how a public supply of electricity in rural areas can be, and is being used.* It was shot on location around Chester with the assistance of S. E. Britton MIEE, Chester's city electrical engineer. It was probably the first publicity film to promote better farming. The film, of over 1000 metres in length, showed both domestic and farm use. It emphasized the value of telephones for obtaining market reports and of wireless for weather forecasts. Half a century ago, the farmer was isolated and relied for information on market day in the local town.

The film showed how an electric motor could work dairy machinery, churn butter, curd cheese, cut chaff, roll meal, saw timber—amongst many other tasks, even to the mowing of the farmhouse lawn. Promotion was not followed by rapid demand. The Electrical Development Association, with S. E. Britton and C. A. Cameron Brown amongst its early pioneers, looked to new applications of electrical power in agriculture. In 1932, several handbooks were published. One dealt with *Electricity in Poultry Farming* and noted that around Kidderminster and Pershore some poultry farmers had introduced 'outdoor foster mothers'. The latter were brooders with low temperature wires set within asbestos boards which, in one case, used in a month only half a unit (costing $1\frac{1}{4}$d per unit) per chick for 2000 chicks. The brooder was mounted 500 millimetres above the floor and, 'for economy of cable runs, these foster mothers should be grouped close together in lines in a sunny spot near the house or source of electricity supply ... farmers who have tried electrical rearing are very satisfied with the results and would not return to the older methods'. This was the forerunner of a new age. Eventually, it became the basis for intensive livestock housing and, its extreme form, the broiler (see Plate 147). At the same time, the EDA noted that in Germany and Holland 'there appear to be possibilities of advantages to be gained from light treatment of plants, chiefly to expedite growth for having flowers ready for an earlier market'. The artificially lit greenhouse was being introduced to stimulate plant growth. Moreover, another EDA paper showed that ploughing and tilling could be undertaken with the Estrade Electrical Haulage Systems and the Rototiller. On heavy soil, some 80×28 metres were tilled in $2\frac{1}{2}$ hours using 13 kWh. These systems did not become widely accepted for field work, though today rotary garden tools are well known.

A year later, in 1933, S. E. Britton gave a paper on 'Five Years Progress in the Electrification of Agriculture around Chester' at the Royal Show at Derby. He quoted from two farms. Oldfields Farm at Fulford used electricity to light the house, yard and buildings and to power barn machinery, pumps, food mixers, incubators, brooders, and dairy equipment. The farm had 120 cows and 6000 hens. Saighton Hall, which was somewhat bigger, used hot water for scalding pigs, for feeding pigs, with a 300 gallon water heater in the dairy, plus motors for cheese vats, cream separation, washing machines, and pumping whey.

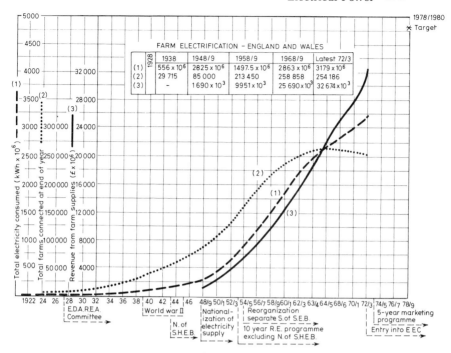

167. FARM ELECTRIFICATION, England and Wales
   (1) Electricity used (kWh × 10⁶)   (2) Total farms connected at end of year
   (3) Revenue from farm supplies (£ × 10⁶)

The Hall had 120 cows, 30 breeding sows and 400 poultry. Consumption increased in three to four years:

	1929	1933
The Oldfields	2270 kWh	27,152 kWh (cost £94)
Saighton Hall	2153 kWh	34,949 kWh (cost £97)

Such examples were exceptional farms. Throughout the 1930s, only about 35,000 farms received electricity in England and Wales.

The Second World War gave impetus to rural electrical distribution and at the time of the nationalization of the industry in 1948 about 6500 farms were being connected annually. In 1953, a ten-year programme was launched to connect 85 per cent of all farms within a decade. The target was reached in 1961 at a cost of £165 m. Thus, this was the period of greatest change in farmstead practice though, for the most part, it made little change in layout or construction. In 1953, the Ministry of Agriculture published a manual on pig housing in which fan ventilation was considered to be experimental. A decade later, environmentally controlled houses were accepted as normal, though not essential, practice.

In 1947, the small electric motor began to replace the steam of the diesel engine around the steading. Elevators for rick building could be powered, as at Jackmans Farm, with a 3-horse-power single truck-type-drive motor (Plate 168). At the same period, new machines were put into old barns. In many cases, conditions were primitive, as with the Bamford Oil Cake Breaker tucked into a corner with the minimum attempt at hygiene (Plate 169). In many farm situations, with dust and straw around, the risk of fire is ever present, even when the wires are in conduit (Plate 170). Though some work areas were more orderly, few gave perfect working conditions. A photograph of 1958 (Plate 171) shows a 10-horse-power, 1430 rpm, LK8 single-phase motor which powered a drive shaft with a series of take-off points for belts to drive barn machinery, including a roller mill and a kibbler. A platform makes storage of prepared feeds easier in lower bins. Lighting of work areas is by a single 40 watt bulb, ladders are simple and work edges unprotected.

Early uses of electrical power made their greatest impact on the small feed-preparation mills and in the cowshed and dairy. Electrical vacuum pulsators, on a hand trolley connected by cable to a power socket, made hand milking almost a thing of the past. The Alfa-Laval milking bucket, with its twin sets of clusters, changed the practice of milk extraction,

168. BUILDING A HAY RICK, Jackmans Farm, Kimbolton, Bedfordshire 1947

169. *(left)* ELECTRIC DRIVE to Bamford Oil Cake Breaker

170. *(right)* CHAFF-CUTTER CONVERTED TO ELECTRIC DRIVE, Great Toteaze Farm, Buxted, Sussex. 1953

171. ELECTRIC-POWERED BARN MACHINERY
1958

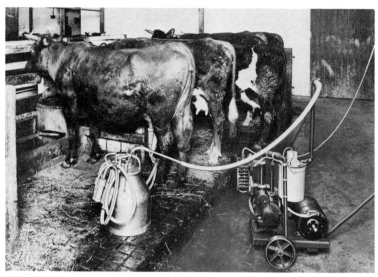

172. BUCKET MILKING in East Suffolk. C. 1950

but not for a decade the layout of the cowshed (Plate 172). Milk passed hygienically from cow to sealed bucket. In model dairies of that time, tasks such as refrigeration and cream separation were conducted in hygienic conditions. Buckets were tipped into churns, which stood on refrigerated banks, and stainless steel began to be used for separation (Plate 173).

Steel tower silos, which began to appear in England in the 1950s, also benefited from electrical power to blow grass into the top of the silo. Plate 174 shows a strange mixture of technology. A horse and cart was used to handle long grass from the field. Two men pitchforked the grass to a cutter and blower, powered by a mobile electric motor, tethered to a stake and cabled up to an electrical supply on a pole, and with a long belt drive between the two machines. The tower silo is an early, totally prefabricated structure. For the first time in farming the distinction between a building and a piece of equipment becomes blurred. Though mechanized, the task of getting grass into a store still used five men.

Such development of electrical power about a quarter of a century ago now seems primitive. Today, almost all farms have a mains electrical supply. A few opt out and prefer to generate their own power from wind or water. Self-sufficiency in farming is likely to attract a fringe of practitioners as energy becomes more expensive and as simple, basic life-styles seem more attractive than urban 'rat-races'. However, in about 1960 the growth of push-button farming began. The control panel for grain-drying plant in Plate 175 reflects a different world from that in the preceding photographs. With elevators and conveyors, grain could

173. (*left*) CREAM SEPARATION. C. 1950. (See also milk cooling, Plate 76)

175. (*right*) GRAIN CONTROL PANEL, Massey Ferguson Butler, Hamptwaril Estate. 1962

174. CHOPPING AND BLOWING GRASS
     c. 1955

176. GRAIN-DRYING AND STORAGE PACKAGE-DEAL UNIT, delt. C. Hurford
1962

be circulated to any storage or drying position at the 'flick of a switch'
(Plate 176).

At the same time, the milking parlours had begun to replace bucket
milking in the cowshed. Work study had shown that the cow should
walk to the man to be milked and that better milking machinery could
be used *in situ* than when carried round by the cowman (Plate 177).
Milk passed direct from the cow to a recording jar before being piped
away to a refrigerated tank in the dairy. The cows were raised so that a
man no longer had to stoop during milking to put on and take off a
cluster. A decade later, all stages of milking except one had become
possible with automation.

In 1974, the National Institute of Agricultural Engineering created a
system which could automatically identify each cow when she entered
a milking parlour. The cow today wears a neckband, marked with her
number (Plate 178). No longer is there a cry:

> Come up Whitefoot, come up Lightfoot;
> Quit the stalks of parsley hollow,
>   Hollow, hollow;
> Come up Jetty, rise and follow,
> From the clovers lift your head;
> Come up Whitefoot, come up Lightfoot,
> Come up Jetty, rise and follow,
> Jetty, to the milking shed.

Jean Ingelow,
The high tide on the coast of Lincolnshire in 1571

The neckband carries a sensor with its numbers as electronic digits
which are picked up by a scanner at the threshold to the parlour. The

177. TANDEM MILKING PARLOUR, Icombe Proper Estates,
Stow-on-the-Wold, Gloucestershire. 1962

178. (*left*) ELECTRONIC COW-IDENTIFICATION SYSTEM. 1974

179. (*right*) ELECTRONIC FEEDING, Ringshall, Suffolk. 1972

recording is transmitted via a computer to an overhead digital recorder,
then to a feeding mechanism at the milking stall, to release a ration
preset against each cow number. This technique is even more advanced
than that installed in 1972 at Chapel Farm, Ringshall, Suffolk (Plate
179). The cowman reads the cow number branded on her rump as she
enters a seventeen-cow, anti-clockwise rotary abreast parlour. The
cowman presses numbers on a console and a preset quantity of liquid

180. SIMULATED-PIG ENVIRONMENTAL RESEARCH. 1974

concentrate is fed to her stall as it rotates for seven minutes while she is milked. In this case, the circular building was formed from vitreous-enamelled steel components normally used for tower silos, 9.4 metres in diameter by 3 metres to the eaves, above which is a reinforced-glass clerestory raked back to a silo cap.

There seems little doubt but that electronics, computers, and auto-mated processes will dominate the farmstead of the future. Genetics and nutrition will be linked and expensive feed and energy inputs will be controlled. As with sensors, the NIAE has researched the control of livestock environment in order to produce better designs for housing (Plate 180). Simulated pigs which emit the temperature and humidity of live animals are placed in full-size, mock-up buildings. Air-ventilation patterns are recorded automatically on film by letting bubbles of helium enter the air inlets to the building. These weave delicate patterns which can be analysed for pig comfort. The design of farm buildings has changed dramatically during the 1970s, largely due to the sophisticated use of electrical energy.

General references

Note This section has been assisted by Mr. P. Wakeford, Head of the Agricultural Section of the Electricity Council (now Farm Electric), and by a paper by Messrs. Bayetto, Paterson & Wakeford for the Institute of Electrical Engineers in 1975.

1. *Electricity Supply in Great Britain: A Chronology*, The Electricity Council, 1977.
2. *Farm Electrification Handbooks*, Electricity Development Association, miscellaneous from 1951.
3. F. E. Rowland, *Electricity in Modern Farming*, Land Books, 1963.

4 Materials and Structure

The materials and construction of the farmstead, within the vernacular tradition, had a close relationship with other rural and village building right up to about 1950. As with other industries, new technologies came into use during the second half of the nineteenth century. The steel-framed Dutch barn was the first example of the standardized, prefabricated farm building. Introduced later was the American precast-concrete stave tower silo. But since 1950, the framed and clad farm building has dominated the steading as much as it has any factory estate. Similarly, though different in scale and in height, prefabricated insulated timber-panel construction has been exploited for small livestock buildings as for small offices, schools and village halls. Building technology on the farm cannot be considered separately from the mainstream of other practice.

This review of farm-building materials and structure has been kept brief. Certainly, it does not attempt to be definitive. However, some definition is desirable of the transition from vernacular to prefabricated construction. This watershed in building design has been as significant as the introduction of diesel and electrical power in production methods. Together they have made a profound though not always desirable impact on rural landscapes.

Scale of building has been changed as well as the formation. Increased building spans, sometimes greater bulk, together with lower roof pitches to serve those spans, mean that many new buildings are out of character with the old steadings. Once buildings do not surround courtyards, their separate linearity shatters the sense of enclosure, of nestling into terrain, of compactness as a landscape feature. These two changes disrupt and destroy the old order, so that in terms of landscape quality, it is far better—though not always desirable from a practical point of view—to divorce the new building from the old steading.

New factory-type farm buildings can be absorbed into the countryside. Choice of location and of siting within that location always remain important. Mass and silhouette, together with scale, need to be considered, though the range of choice may be restricted in relation to functional need. In relation to location, but allowing for the requirement of the size of enclosed space, a decision has to be made whether the new building must be—or should be—dominant or recessive within the landscape. From this decision will stem the right selection of colours and of textures for materials. These materials do not have to be vernacular. Modern profiled claddings can be suitable provided that colour and texture relate to the surroundings. Detail, as in all building, is important, particularly the co-ordination of services and attachments with the building structure and the surrounding yards, fences, and other equipment. In most situations there needs to be definition, from the mid-distance, between the various external planes of a building, especially between walls and roof. Buildings need to be recognized by their shape and not by their silhouette. Colour—as well as weathering—may achieve this distinction. Shadows at eaves and verge may enhance it.

Landscape is an essential part of the way we see buildings. Their relation to contour, to folds in the terrain, and to vegetation is important. The mass of related features in the landscape, as seen from various viewpoints, can be spread over a wide area. Features half a mile apart, or even over several miles, may well have a relationship within our field of vision. Therefore, tree planting does not always have to be immediately adjacent to a building to be effective. Depending on locality, the canvas can be broad. Equally important are the elevation of viewpoint and its distance. There is a vital difference in the effect of the proportional mass of buildings seen in a plateau or from upland into valley.

Unfortunately, for reasons outside the scope of this book, though the message about good design is simple, we all witness too often that it has not been heeded. The modern steading seldom makes an aesthetic contribution to the landscape equal to that which our generation inherited.

Vernacular

Local building, using indigenous materials, evolved its own styles according to local custom handed down through craftsmen. Custom stemmed from experience and this was based on three main factors—structural limitations, climate, and agricultural need.

All materials have different structural properties. Over centuries of use, their potential is exploited as experience is gained. Therefore, as long as materials come from a local area, there may be marked characteristics of local style. Britain is noted for its close knit geological variations so that, in many parts, there can be extreme differences of material within a radius of twenty miles. This is as true for farm building as it is for other village structures. Windmills provide a particularly notable example. Timber construction gave rise to the post and smock mills. But where timber was short, the brick tower-mill became the norm (see Plate 92), being very different in style.

In timber construction, there was a significant change in the seventeenth century. Centuries of over-use of oak, intensified by the Elizabethan naval requirements, had reduced oakwoods so that their timber was only for the rich to use. Elm, too, had been exploited. Thus, medieval barns, such as that at Wendens Ambo (Plate 198) with its magnificent structural timbers, became a rarity. Most Georgian barns, even in timbered areas, were meaner in construction, using timbers more prone to decay. By Regency times, imported scantlings of Douglas fir and other softwoods from America and, later, from Scandinavia, changed techniques again. Thus, barns and watermills, such as that at Alton (Plate 85), were constructed of imported timbers, especially when close to the main docks.

It was the growth of international trade via the expanding ports, later intensified by the rapid extension of the canal and railway networks, that put an end to the vernacular tradition. Nothing changed nineteenth-century architectural shape more than the handling of Welsh and Belgian slates throughout much of Britain. Thatch required roofs pitched at 55° to 60°, plain tile at 45° to 55°, and even pantile not much under 35°. But slate gave the possibility of sound roofs at 25° and even lower. Thus, alien roof silhouettes began to appear throughout the country. The same kind of change occurred elsewhere in the world as the first steps towards 'international styles' of building were taken.

It is true that in earlier times there was some mix of materials. In cathedrals, Caen stone and Purbeck marble were much sought after and even Stonehenge was imported from Wales. For humbler buildings, near ports, materials were often imported as ballast. Into East Anglia came the Belgian black-glazed pantile (Plate 199) and the distinctive Belgian brick, to mix with the reds of the local clay, both being imported as ballast against the bales of wool exported from the great flocks of Tudor prosperity. For probably much the same reason, the alien 'Dutch' stepped gable became a familiar feature in parts of East Anglia.

The erosion of the vernacular tradition in the steading, as in the village, was intensified as soon as transport became cheap. The mis-named 'corrugated tin' became the farmer's best friend. Profiled, gal-vanized sheets were used to clad steel and timber framed buildings. Old barns, requiring repair to thatch or tile or boards, were stripped and clad with the new material. New buildings could have low-pitched roofs and, since the material was light, their spans could be increased from one rod (that is about 5 metres), which was a normal module, to any dimension. With lattice trusses and, later, with portal frames, clear spans of 60 feet (about 18 metres) were particularly economic. When lean-to roofs were attached, the overall width of the building could become 120 feet (36 metres). And the umbrella provided was cheap. In the same manner, the ubiquitous hollow concrete block was used for 'strong' walls rather than brick or stone. Throughout Britain, indeed throughout much of the world, farm buildings now use the same basic materials, often looking like any other small factory. With the exploita-tion of the Rhodesian and Canadian asbestos mines, asbestos-cement profiled sheets seemed to stretch round the industrial world.

Climate as well as materials affected the detail of all vernacular building. The wide, snow-protecting eaves of Switzerland (see Plate 21) are an example. Indeed, strong eaves are a feature of all wet climates since this is a point of great weakness. Cast-iron guttering, to carry rain-water away, was a Victorian invention, and projections to throw water away from weak places, such as window and door openings, were normal practice. Even in barns, where detail was kept economic, hood moulds and string courses were used, though less frequently and less richly than in houses. The midstrey eaves detail is a particular feature (see Plate 198), sometimes repeated in modern construction. Methods of ventilating stock and crop buildings varied according to the humidity and the wind levels of various regions. In this, agricultural requirements begin to influence building design, making steadings different from other building types.

Cross ventilation to hay barns is vital and, to a lesser extent, to corn barns. Damp, warm produce has a point of instantaneous combustion. Many a barn or rick has burnt when no naked light has been around. Fire is a major hazard, producing its own influence on building layout (see page 72). But the wall holes formed to provide ventilation had their own regional patterns and, in their own way, evolved as a decorative detail (see Plate 200). In stock buildings, draught-free ventilation has always been a vital feature. Air currents must be deflected and wind speed reduced. This has led to a variety of baffled air inlets, hopper windows and, more recently, to space boarding.

This is not a book about vernacular construction. A detailed study of farm building and the evolution of building technique to fulfil its particular functions has yet to be made. Mechanical handling methods, discussed here, have influenced design and construction, but many other features would be worth further examination. For example, keeping milk cool is an essential requirement. The timber lattice window of the traditional farmhouse dairy can still be seen around the countryside (Plate 111). The Victorian model farm often had an octagonal dairy with conical roof, vented at the top. Windows were shuttered and interiors would be lined with decorative glazed tiles. Around the exterior would be planted yew trees, often in a radial pattern. These gave perpetual shade to the dairy and also, to some extent, acted as an insect repellent. Sometimes, a little to the south, a forest tree, oak or beech, would be planted so that it, too, could cast its great shadow over the dairy. The creation of controlled micro-climates is an essential part of farm building design.

Prefabricated Structure

Prefabrication for farm equipment is an old idea. As already shown, the Chinese prefabricated sickle blades at the time when the Greek civilization was just beginning (Plate 97). Timber buildings were prefabricated for the Roman army, being based on modular framed construction as at the Lunt granary (Plate 196). Field machinery began to be prefabricated during the eighteenth century when the first agricultural workshops began to acquire national names (see page 124).

In one sense most buildings, other than those of rammed soil or *in situ* concrete, are prefabricated. Bricks, stones and timber scantlings are preformed off the site. The medieval hive-stand, now re-erected at Hartpury (Plate 181), shows a type of 'prefabrication': stone blocks,

181. BEE-HIVE STAND, Hartpury College of Agriculture, Gloucestershire, re-erected 1974

slabs, partitions and slates have a modular rhythm. There are two shelves, each holding fourteen hives, divided by stone slabs. These are contained over a structure of five main bays. There are, however, four bays to the ridge tiles, so there is a certain lack of co-ordination. It is thought that the structure, known as a bee bole, which came from Nailsworth, but was of Caen stone, had originally been for the manor of Minchinhampton, producing both honey and beeswax. The bees had 'front doors' through the solid flank of the stand and the attendant reached the honey away from their flight path. It is a rare type of farm building. Specialized buildings, especially of timber, are suitable for prefabrication. Lugar in his *The Country Gentleman's Architect* of 1807

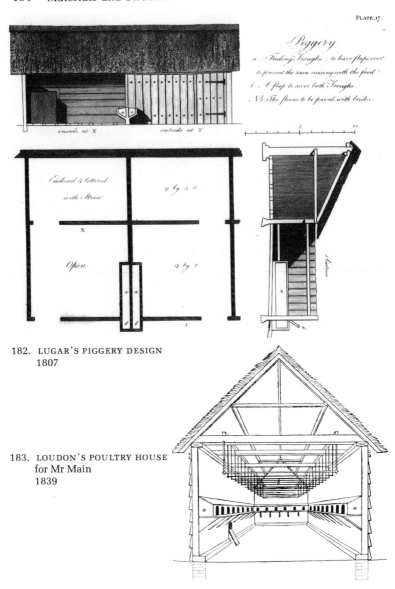

Piggery

*a Feeding Troughs . . to have flaps over
to prevent the rain mixing with the food
b . A flap to cover both Troughs .
N.3. The floors to be paved with bricks.*

182. LUGAR'S PIGGERY DESIGN
1807

183. LOUDON'S POULTRY HOUSE
for Mr Main
1839

shows a simple sty in which walls, gates, flooring, etc., are from regular
planks set to a frame to suit their basic width (Plate 182). Loudon in his
Encyclopædia of 1839 suggests a similar possibility of prefabrication in
his arrangements for rows of laying boxes and hanging perches for
poultry (Plate 183).

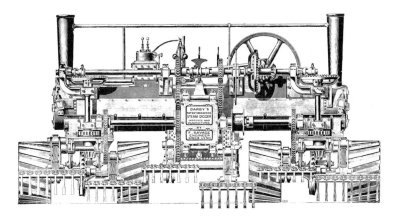

184. DARBY'S BROADSIDE STEAM DIGGER

The complexity of nineteenth-century machinery made standardization in manufacture essential. Components had to be drawn in detail before fabrication. Darby's steam digger, made by Savage of King's Lynn, shows how precision was essential (Plate 184).

Naturally, the same philosophy began to be applied to the manufacture of steel buildings. The Dutch barn was perhaps the first and, in the 1880s, other buildings such as those for silage began to be prefabricated. But, in the main, traditional building construction was the norm for most farm buildings right into the 1950s. This tended to mean farm operations had to work within narrow spans or, with steel trusses, multiples of such spans and internal stanchions. If any single person could be thought to have influenced the early development of prefabricated farm buildings, it must be A. J. Hosier, a farmer turned engineer. He established a profitable form of extensive farming on the thin pastures of the Wiltshire chalk downs. Extensive systems depend on large areas with low capital expenditure and low output. Hosier had some 400 hectares previously thought of as sheepland. Having small herds set to several farmsteads would have needed heavy investment in fixed equipment. Milking machines were essential to reduce labour and Hosier invented a portable milking shed, known as a bail, which could be moved to different parts of the downland to milk batches of cows. This was in 1922 and five years later Hosier marketed his bail and founded a major agricultural company. At the same time, he put an end to the prevailing idea that farming had to have buildings with foundations and tiled roofs. The metal 'box' had arrived within which many tasks could be conducted cheaply. With the bail, the cows went to the man to be milked, unlike in the cowshed where the man had to go from stall to stall. By the 1950s, the side-by-side or abreast arrangement for

185. HOSIER CHUTE BAIL
1964

186. DIAGRAM OF
BASIC MILKING PARLOURS
1964

Key

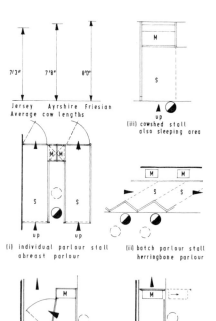

milking position

milk recording jar

M manger

S stall

cow route

7'3" 7'8" 8'0"

Jersey Ayrshire Friesian
Average cow lengths

M

S

up
(iii) cowshed stall
also sleeping area

M   M

S   S

up   up

(i) individual parlour stall
abreast parlour

M   M

S   S

(ii) batch parlour stall
herringbone parlour

M

S   PIT

(i) individual parlour stall
tandem parlour

M

S   PIT

(ii) batch parlour stall
chute parlour

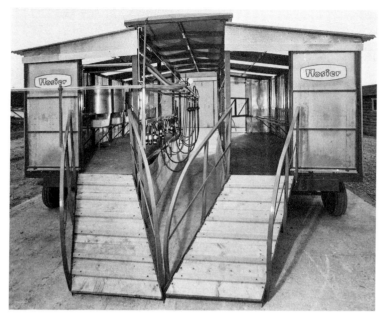

187. HOSIER HERRINGBONE BAIL. 1964

milking positions had changed to the in-line, chute, or tandem arrangement. The cowman milked at three or four points and the cows moved through the building or bail from end to end (Plates 185 and 186).

Milking became more sophisticated in the 1960s. Herringbone milking layouts were invented in New Zealand in the 1950s and introduced to Europe a decade later. By letting the cows stand in raked alignment so their rumps were angled to the cowman, he could milk four cows to each side of him. He did not have to walk as far as in the chute arrangement. Moreover, two-level milking had become the normal practice so that the cowman no longer had to stoop. Whilst four cows gave their milk into the pipeline, the cowman washed and prepared the cows to the other side. Though the herringbone was a more complex structure, Hosier's firm were not deterred and it too became mobile (Plate 187).

Throughout the 1950s, more and more types of farm buildings became prefabricated as mobile or fixed equipment. The Ministry of Agriculture coined the phrase 'fixed equipment' on the farm for all structures during this period. The word 'building' was no longer adequate to describe the range of storage, processing and production structures arriving on the farm from factories. The corrugated metal sheet could be used for many functions besides roofing. Bins of the kind

188. GALVANIZED CYLINDRICAL GRAIN BINS (see also Plates 51 and 52) 1964

in Plate 188 are difficult to describe as buildings. Some equipment, such as that for milking, had a particular purpose, but many units of equipment, with or without a building type of enclosure, could be sold for any function.

A containing crate in which a sow could farrow and suckle without crushing her litter had been devised in the 1950s (Plate 189). Crushed piglets when sows farrowed in pens had been a major problem. The idea of selling as a package the crate, the surrounding creep areas for the piglets, complete with raised floor of rubber matting and mesh around the sow, and of bedded area with heater lamp for the piglets, all set within low walls of compressed asbestos-cement boards, showed how diverse the concept of prefabrication could be.

Prefabrication, as with Meccano, permits some flexibility during construction to create one-off solutions. The Hosier bail was a package bought like a tractor. It was delivered complete and ready to use. The broiler sheds which were developed during the 1950s also were sold as a package deal in which building and equipment came as one unit of sale (Plate 190). Only the foundation and floor, and the link-up of services, required normal sitework. All other components came ready to be fixed on to the base. Throughout the 1960s, the package-deal building became the norm for nearly all types of farm management.

Cows from time immemorial had been housed and milked in stalls in cowsheds. In winter, they stayed for months chained into their stalls. In summer, they grazed nearby pastures but had to return twice a day to the stalls to be milked. The milking bail and later, as fixed equipment, the milking parlour, changed this. During the 1950s cows were housed in winter loose on deep litter straw, in what were known as bedded yards. In many cases, the portal-framed building giving wide, clear spans of 20 metres or more were suitable for this purpose, with a small adjacent structure for the parlour and dairy. Self-feeding of silage was introduced. Silage was sometimes kept in unroofed clamps, sometimes in silobarns. Later, in the 1960s, it might be kept in tower silos, being distributed to mangers on an automated and rationed basis. Again, there was change. In the early 1960s, a Welsh farmer, Howell Evans, invented the cubicle for housing the cow. Each cow had her own cubicle—established by the custom of a pecking order—which she could lie in when she wished. At other times, she was free to walk around passageways or go to the silobarn. With the development of cubicle housing, the package-deal system established a new market (Plate 191).

Today, all types of crop and stock building are available as package-deal systems. Many are available on a hire-purchase basis, like other products. In some cases, especially with pig houses, not only are the building and finance provided by the manufacturer but the feed

189. (*left*) FARROWING CRATE. 1973

191. (*right*) HILLSPAN PACKAGE-DEAL CUBICLE HOUSE. 1970

190. PACKAGE-DEAL BROILER SHED. 1960

192.
LAMBERT-GEERKENS
PIGGERY,
delivered from
Belgium to England
1974

company provides pigmeal as part of the deal. In a few cases, the supply of weaners for fattening to bacon weight is also in the contract. The farmer only has to provide daily management.

There are still one-off farm buildings designed. They may be for prestige, or because the farmer has a particular interest in his own management techniques which do not conform to the package concept. Many are due to part-adaptation of existing buildings or because the farmer wants to build his own buildings. But the trend is towards factory-made buildings. They can be distributed around the world and sold like cars (Plate 192).

The problem, in terms of landscape and design, of cheap, mass-produced farm buildings has been of concern to many national organizations such as the Design Council and the Council for the Protection of Rural England. The former has published reports on tower silos, colour claddings, and components. The latter published a report in 1974 on *Development Control: Package Buildings*. This pointed out that once a building became an assembly of parts in a package deal then its basic design was predetermined at the prototype stage. Good design depends on trained disciplines being available at the drawing-board study stage.

The Container

One function of the farmstead is to hold—or contain—produce. It will be held until needed for consumption by livestock or by the household. It may be held for sale and, as harvest may create a glut, until market prices have risen. In this way, farmers 'play the market'. In most cases, the aim is to hold the produce in the minimum container structurally possible which permits filling and emptying the store.

Throughout the world corn or, when ground, meal has been contained in many types of silo or bin. The Ancient Egyptians had their

193. SILO, River Volta

195. SILOS at Tacoleche, Mexico

194. SILO, Sudan

domed bunkers (Plate 133). The earth pot on legs can be found in many parts of Africa. Their form is timeless, being known throughout recorded history (Plates 193 and 194). In Mexico, at least since the Spaniards settled, conical silos have been erected to hold grain (Plate 195).

196. RECONSTRUCTED HORREA at Lunt Fort, Baginton, near Coventry

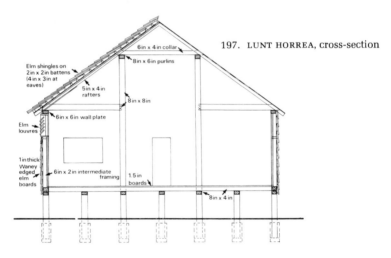

197. LUNT HORREA, cross-section

Elm shingles on 2 in x 2 in battens (4 in x 3 in at eaves)

6 in x 4 in collar

8 in x 6 in purlins

5 in x 4 in rafters

8 in x 8 in

6 in x 6 in wall plate

Elm louvres

1 in thick Waney edged elm boards

6 in x 2 in intermediate framing

1.5 in boards

8 in x 4 in

In cold northern Europe, grain was kept on its straw for long sessions of winter threshing and, therefore, barns were required more than silos (see page 117). The Romans had grain barns. A reconstruction of such a barn was made at the Lunt Roman fort at Baginton, near Coventry, in 1975 (Plates 196 and 197). Such stores had raised floors and perforated walls to provide ventilation and to restrict vermin; they were known as horrea (Plate 134). The horrea at Lunt contained enough grain for a cohort of 480 men for a year and records show that average rations were 7 hundredweight. Thus, the store had to hold about 170 tonnes of grain and this was in a row of centre bins, 3 × 3 metres, flanked by walkways, and other bins 3 × 1½ metres at the side walls. Bins would be filled about 1½ metres deep. These buildings would have been erected by Roman engineers within about two weeks since the timber frames were

198. TIMBER AND THATCH BARN, Wendens Ambo, Essex
17th century

199. FLINT-AND-CLUNCH AND PANTILE TITHE BARN, Dersingham, Norfolk
17th century

200. VENTILATED STORAGE BARN ABOVE COWSHED, Freuchelerly, Belgium
18th century

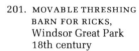

201. MOVABLE THRESHING
BARN FOR RICKS,
Windsor Great Park
18th century

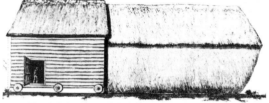

prefabricated on a 3 × 1½ metres module. In medieval Europe, barns became permanent structures of some size to hold the whole-crop. They became a landscape feature (see Plates 2 and 101). They are most photogenic due to their simple shapes and vernacular, weathered materials, and there were many variations on the theme. On the Continent, two-floored buildings were quite normal, with storage set above the livestock (Plate 200). In the eighteenth century, there was a portable, wheeled threshing barn in Windsor Great Park (Plate 201). In the Netherlands, ricks and barns have had the characteristic shape of the Dutch barn (Plate 62). But their square barns also were distinctive, anyway from the late eighteenth century (Plates 202 and 203). It was a form of construction not so dissimilar to the great storehouses or larders known in Iceland and the northern islands (Plate 204). Some were built over excavated cellars. In Greenland they were of stone. The fatabur, or larder, is mentioned in the sagas.

In Northern America, the gambrel roof or mansard shape of barn became a particular feature of the farmstead. Its origins are obscure. It seemed to spread from New York State following settlement by the Dutch in the seventeenth century, though its particular kinked roof

202.   DUTCH BOARDED SQUARE BARN

204.   FATABUR, Thorshavn, Faroes

203.   DUTCH PANTILED SQUARE BARN

205. MANSARD BARN, Lac St. Augustin, Quebec. 1810

does not seem to derive from the Netherlands. However, the Dutch had always had hay storage under high, thatched roofs, set above the mow-floor level and taken up to the eaves. The gambrel shape gave the same facilities and, with softwood construction from the American pine and spruce, it may have been from functional necessity of using shorter lengths of timber. The barn shown in Plate 205 was built for M. Goulet in 1810, measuring some 38 × 8 metres, and it is reputed to be the finest in the province. It is so tightly sealed, with butt-jointed plank walls and coved mansard roof, that there is a special cat-hole under the second window. The building includes storage barn, threshing floor and cattlehouse.

The revolution in storage containers came with the steel-framed Dutch barn and the vertical silo of reinforced concrete. Tower silos were

206. TIMBER SILAGE WALLS AND BARN, Portways Farm, Cuckfield, Sussex 1960

207. OLD AND NEW TOWER SILOS, Wappingthorn Farm, Steyning, Sussex

for storage of mown grass which was allowed to ferment under compression to form silage. Originally, a silo was a pit in the ground to hold grain. But in the nineteenth century, to ensile became common for roots and green fodder for livestock. The practice was widespread by 1875 and Horace Cox reviewed the substantial progress in the new science in his book of 1885 on the subject. A French farmer engineer, M. Auguste Goffart, designed many masonry clamps with walls 4 metres or 5 metres high and which supported an open timber frame, trusses and tiled roofs. In some cases, the clamps were partly below ground and the grass was compacted by horses. Viscomte Arthur de Chezelles, at Liancourt St. Pierre, built such a silo for 1500 tonnes and some 65 × 6 metres in area around 1880. A few years later a number of prefabricated, circular wooden silos were on the market and Bentalls, the Essex engineers, were selling concrete silos with walls 75 millimetres thick and up to 7.5 metres high. Grass was chopped by steam power and then winched to the top for filling. It was compacted by placing a layer of stones over it – some nine tonnes to each chamber, 3.3 × 3.3 metres square. It was common on the Continent and spread to America. Thorold Rogers wrote of silage in 1883 in his *Ensilage in America*: 'Much is yet to be done in *americanising* the whole matter and we have no doubt that the experiments now being made will greatly simplify not only the building of the silo but every *other* step in this method.'

The silage clamp, whether above or below ground, has been a practical method of storing wet grass instead of wilted hay. The Americans created the tower silo as early as the 1880s. It was of *in situ*, reinforced concrete. Several were built in England in the 1920s. They went out of favour a generation later since they were time consuming to load and difficult to unload. By the time prefabricated towers came in during the

208. SEVEN STAVED TOWERS, Lincolnshire. 1966

1940s in America and the early 1960s in England, the earlier towers were redundant. Their diameters and heights were too small to make good silage. In the 1920s—as later—towers were thought to be an intrusion in the landscape. Many were castellated. The two at Wappingthorn Farm were formed as an entrance, a fortified gateway, into the steading (Plate 207). It was designed in 1928 by Maxwell Ayrton, father to the more famous sculptor, Michael Ayrton. Wappingthorn would have pleased Sanderson Miller, the eighteenth-century landscape architect, who declared: 'Let every structure needful for a farm arise in castle semblance.'

The modern tower silos of precast-concrete staves or of galvanized or stove-enamelled steel plates gave a boost to vertical storage. Grass was blown in at the top and, mostly, also unloaded automatically from the top downwards via an external chute (Plate 37). Some, hermetically

209. TWO STOVE-ENAMELLED TOWERS, Essex

210. WET GRAIN 100-TONNE SILO
1962

sealed, had bottom unloaders. In the 1960s, towers were only used for wet or partly wilted grass. In Lincolnshire, Oliver Simon was one of the first farmers to ensile whole-crop barley for his cattle (Plate 208). By this method, barley was harvested green, like grass, and provided more nutrients than conventional silage. The bigger of his seven towers were for this purpose. Hermetically sealed towers, in contrast, could be used either for grass or for undried grain. Thus, two 350-tonne wet-grain towers could be combined with a 'conventional' grain drying/storage plant on an Essex farm (Plate 209). However, most wet-grain stores tended to be much squatter (Plate 210).

For human consumption, grain is used at 14 to 16 per cent moisture content, but for livestock the grain for rolled barley must be at least 18 per cent and, hermetically, can be stored at 25 per cent moisture content. This is of great advantage in wet harvesting seasons. Always there are variations on a theme. Butyl rubber sheets have been used for lining lagoons and slurry compounds. In 1968, sheets, restrained by Weld-mesh rolls 2½ metres high, were formed in bunkers of 20 metres diameter with 40 degree cones, and were inflated (Plate 211). Wet grain was blown in until the store was full, when the container was allowed to deflate. Each store held about 750 tonnes and, being sealed hermetically, deflation by suction killed off pests.

Prefabricated, galvanized-steel grain bins became widely used in the 1950s, either as single units (Plate 52) or as nests, as they are known, with rectangular bins bolted together under a self-supporting roof (Plate 209). But during the 1960s it was found possible and cheaper to blow grain on to the floor of a barn and to dry it via a series of prefabricated ducts. Some stores had fan chambers to provide the air flow, positioned at the end of the main 'A'-duct (Plate 212). In some, a portable, low-volume aerator could be attached to the ends of the laterals (Plate 213).

Grain or meal needs to be handled quickly to suit modern haulage. To resist the tendency of granular materials to dome or to funnel (Plate 214), thus blocking the outlet movement, bins need steeply raked sides (Plates 215 and 216).

Farming became an industrial process with the second agricultural revolution. Produce, such as potatoes and grain, can be handled by pallet and fork-lift truck as in other factories (Plate 217). Pallets do not need conventional storage buildings (Plate 218). Containers, for produce, both for storage and for processing, are a natural structure for mechanized farms. Livestock, too, can be contained in much the same way as produce. The requirements are similar if reduced to the simple logistics of food production. The animals can be held in small crates, stacked together like pallets. Water and feed can be conveyed in and muck (and, with hens, eggs) conveyed out. The caged-bird system of egg production, later known as battery houses, started in California in

211. (right) INFLATABLE CHERWELL
GRAIN STORE
1968

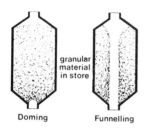

granular
material
in store

Doming   Funnelling

214. DOMING AND FUNNELLING

212. (above, left) VENTILATED
FLOOR GRAIN STORAGE,
main 'A'-duct and
vented laterals

213. (above, right) LATERAL
VENTILATION TO
FLOOR STORE

215. (right) NEST OF TWELVE
RAISED 10-TONNE BINS
1960

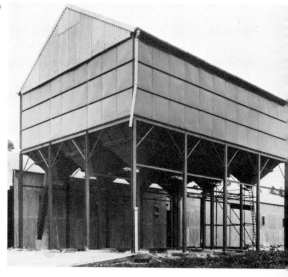

216. PIG-MEAL BINS FILLED BY TANKER. 1962

217. PALLET GRAIN in Holland
1961

218. PALLET POTATOES
stored without a barn

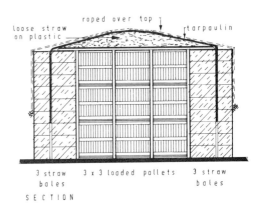

loose straw
on plastic

roped over top

tarpaulin

3 straw
bales

3 x 3 loaded pallets

3 straw
bales

SECTION

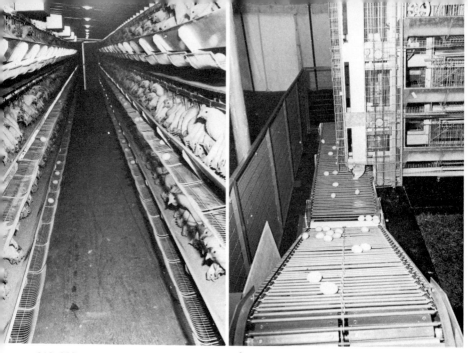

219, 220. THREE-TIER BATTERY HOUSE and EGG CONVEYOR TO BATTERY HOUSE. 1968

the 1940s. During the 1950s, it became a principal system throughout the civilized world.

The Future

There are so many pressures, political and technical, on the process of food production that its technology is difficult to forecast. This is true both in the field and in the steading.

Food production is likely to become more standardized. Therefore, buildings, too, will relate to specific performance and management specifications. There will be fewer individual designs. At present, many farmers plead, with some justification, that their individual farm system is a special case, but as has happened with poultry, systems will tend to become more clear-cut and buildings more recognizably related to a known system. On the other hand, building is costly and self-sufficiency farming is on the increase. Therefore, within certain types of farming, it is possible that do-it-yourself building, including its design, will continue to flourish.

The need for cheap food is paramount. The broiler, twelve weeks old, and the steak, twelve months old, fill the supermarket shops. They require specialized buildings planned to fulfil a regular contract of young stock fattened to slaughter within precise food-conversion and growth rates. At the same time there is a rapid growth of wholefood

221. PEASANT FARMING AND DOVECOTE, Mykonos, Greece

shops for which produce takes longer to grow, has more flavour, comes from more traditional types of management and building, and costs more. The tradition of peasant farming, self-sufficient and poor, using buildings of vernacular materials, will continue and even find some new adherents (Plate 221).

Buildings will be prefabricated in factories, often being sold and erected within a package service. These factories may be owned by national, even inter-national companies. Some of the latter may be under a vertically integrated ownership; that is the building manufacturer, the service industry for livestock and livestock feed, the processor and even the retailer to the customer, may all be one company. Such companies already exist: Unilever Ltd., who not only own the sausage producers, the Walls Meat Company, but also several pig farms, provide but one example. Against this, is the influential modern philosophy that we should accept that small is beautiful.

Buildings will continue to be designed for rapid obsolescence to permit rapid changes in the demand for convenience and fashion foods and to allow for rapid changes of technology. Both have been the hallmark of the last three decades. The throw-away society has its fascination, but the energy crisis may make conservation of building materials more critical. We may again, as in the past, build for prosperity expecting management to be stable within defined techniques.

Materials handling will be essential to reduce manual labour and to

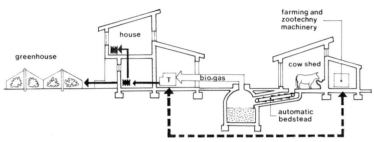

222. INTEGRATED POWER, Total Energy Module (TOTEM)

223. EAST COAST GRAIN STORAGE, Diss, Norfolk

permit a short working week in all branches of food production, including milk production. Diesel and electricity will still be the power source to permit automation, and databanks and computers will organize most of the routines, but alternative power sources from sun, wind and water will become commonplace and most wastes will be recycled. Some buildings will be powered from waste materials. Fiat launched their concept of TOTEM in 1980 in which bio-gas produced from livestock waste could provide a primary source of energy to heat a range of buildings from dwellings to greenhouses (Plate 222). Thus new types of structure on the farm will be evolved. There may well be a central area to process power. Though, generally, manual and routine work will be eliminated, there will be other types of farm where people seek the satisfaction of manual, craft work.

Farm buildings may no longer be on farms. There is little reason why produce is stored and processed on the farm. The agricultural industrial estate, close to road-rail links, could become commonplace. A 10,000-tonne storage unit completed in 1980 extended a range of grain storage for East Coast Grain Ltd., being constructed from the inception of the company over several years by Grain Storage (Norfolk) Ltd. This plant demonstrates how a corn region may have its buildings centralized away from the farmland near road-rail links (Plate 223). Isolated, small groups of buildings have some inefficiencies. But, again, there is a social desire for more people to part-time farm, to community farm, or to self-sufficiency farm. Similarly, the mixing of food production and recreation, at least in the less fertile districts, will increase.

Thus the only certainty that can be stated is that society itself is in a state of flux. There can be no certainty as to the type of building required to serve such a society. What does seem probable is that farming will evolve towards a clear polarity. There will be within high technology, many centrally organized, internationally directed food production systems. Buildings will be factories. At the same time there will be an undercurrent of intermediate technology, peasant-type farming systems where the style of life is valued. It is anyone's guess. I expect in the 1980s and 1990s a ratio of 4:1 between high and intermediate systems in terms of food produced and of 1:4 in terms of the agricultural working population in such systems.

Glossary

Abreast parlour The original milking parlour in which the stalls are placed side-by-side, with each pair divided by a feed hopper and an operator's work space. Cows enter a stall from the rear and exit via a head gate. Stalls may be at floor level or raised up one or two steps above the entrance and work area.

Aerofoil An elliptical steel foil, usually of shaped narrow blades set within an helical arc, and designed to spin rapidly due to wind pressure, thereby turning a spindle which can power machinery or generate electricity.

Aerogenerator Wind pressure harnessed by revolving collectors, blades or sails, being designed to turn into and with wind movements, and being used to generate electricity.

Apex hut An ark for loose-range poultry constructed with a timber A-frame; some can be larger, semi-permanent, and placed on a concrete platform.

Arable farm Ploughed and tilled land, probably with rotational crops, and farmed without livestock, thus requiring artificial fertilizers unless organic wastes are imported from other farms. Arable farms are usually large to justify the field equipment.

Ark A portable field hut or shelter, capable of being moved by two men, mainly used in paddocks in extensive farming systems for rearing pigs or poultry. Usually constructed of timber, set on skids for ease of transport, but may be formed simply from curved sheets of galvanized steel.

Auger A long, rotating screw, powered by a motor, set in a galvanized-steel cylinder, and used to raise and convey granular materials such as corn or feed but sometimes for semi-solids such as slurry: most are easily carried by two men, but longer ones may be mounted on small, wheeled trivods.

Baconer house A building used to fatten weaners until they reach bacon weight at around 100 kilograms. Many different layouts of house, from semi-open to total environmental control, can prove acceptable depending on management.

Bail A portable milking parlour, originated as an abreast type by Hosier in Wiltshire to suit extensive dairy farming on the Downs. Today, herringbone bails are available and suit outlying herds.

Balk A regional term for a partitioned loft or platform, usually those in small, outlying cattle shelters.

Barn The main storage building for farm crops, particularly cereals (from OE 'bern' or barley house), traditionally built as one large compartment to take the total harvest from one farm. Access was via the midstrey (q.v.).

Battery house A building to house laying hens in cages or batteries, usually stacked in three or four decks of wired compartments, and often being fully automated with conveyors for feeding, cleaning and egg collection. Most houses have fully controlled environments and may be grouped in large units. This intensive management system led to the description 'factory farming'.

Bedded yard An enclosed, or part-open, yard for livestock to lie down on bedding in which the dung is mixed as it falls, being covered at intervals with fresh bedding so that anaerobic action takes place and the bedding becomes warm and not rank. Cattle yards over a full winter can create a bed of up to 1.5 metres depth. The manure can be spread on land prior to ploughing as organic fertilizer.

Bedding Most bedding is of straw from cereal farms, though other materials such as bracken, jute, leaves, sawdust, shavings, or shredded paper have been used, as have thick rubber mats.

Bee bole A wall recess, or sometimes recess compartments in special stone structures, in which skeps used to be placed to act as a bee hive.

Bin A container, usually for feed or grain, sometimes of plywood, but usually of galvanized steel, and either circular or square. The latter may interlock to form a 'nest'. Bins may be inside a barn or may support their own roof. Ventilated bins, with a perforated floor over a plenum, may be used for drying grain. Bins can be filled and emptied mechanically.

Binder A field machine used to bind harvested cereal crops, but now superseded by the combine harvester.

Bothy A Gaelic term for a single-room building for a farm labourer, often a stockman at a steading or at an outlying shelter.

Broiler house An environmentally controlled building to house broilers, that is poultry fattened from day-old chicks for about ten weeks, and usually in groups of 5000–10,000 per house with wood shavings as bedding and with feeding fully automated.

Brooder house An environmentally controlled building to house brooders, that is to rear chicks for replacement stock, either in cages or in pens.

Buckrake An attachment, invented by Patterson, to a tractor's hydraulic forearms, being a rake with long tines used to lift mown grass into a clamp.

Bulk floor store A framed building with retaining walls, possibly with ducts for drying, and used to store crops, particularly grain, in bulk on the floor.

Bulk tank A refrigerated tank of stainless steel or fibreglass used to cool and to store milk on the farm, being filled from the parlour by pipeline and being emptied by a Milk Marketing Board or dairy road-tanker.

Bunker silo A horizontal clamp of simple construction for grass silage.

Bushel An historic measure for grain containing 4 pecks or 8 gallons.

Byre A regional term for a cowshed.

Cake Compressed, concentrated cattle food, usually in cubes, sometimes in cakes or blocks, being ground barley plus additives such as minerals, molasses, vitamins, etc., to provide a 'whole food' less roughage.

Cartshed An open-fronted building, facing away from the sun, and used to house the farm carts and wagons: sometimes now referring to any implement shed.

Cattle grid A grating of horizontal bars or girders, let into and across a farm road, usually to dispense with a gate at a fence or hedge, and in which the grid is spaced to permit boots or vehicles to have passage but to be impassable for hooved stock.

Cellar A reception pit under a perforated floor which collects slurry until emptied. Shallow pits are emptied by sluice or by suction; deep cellars on a sloping site may be emptied by tractor plus scoop from the lower level.

Chaff The husk of the corn separated after threshing and winnowing.

Chitting house A building in which seed potato chits or germinates: either a glass-house or a windowless shed lit by tubular lights. The seed is stored in slatted trays until ready for planting.

Churn A tall, galvanized-steel container and lid, usually holding 10 gallons, in which cooled milk was stored before bulk tanks.

Churn stand A platform at lorry height, often at the roadside near the farm gate, on which milk churns were placed for daily collection.

Chute parlour A milking parlour in which the cows stand in stalls, head-to-tail, alongside the operator's pit, each stall having a feed trough. Cows enter and leave each chute as a batch.

Clamp A horizontal crop store, usually with a concrete floor. Potato clamps are insulated and protected by mud and straw over the roots. Beet and other root clamps are left uncovered. Grass-silage clamps, or bunkers, have retaining walls to two or three sides and may be set in excavated ground to reduce cost, but most today are above ground for better quality control. Grass may be stored long, chopped or lacerated. Grass is best pre-wilted to reduce moisture and it should be covered by weighted plastic sheets after compaction by the tractor driving on top of the clamp. An air-tight clamp is best, preferably vacuum sealed.

Cluster The four vacuum-operated teat cups formed in a cluster to discharge into one pipeline as used in mechanical milking.

Collecting yard An open or roofed yard into which a milking herd is collected prior to milking and opening direct into a parlour. Yards may be rectangular, wedge shaped or circular.

Combine harvester A self-propelled machine which both harvests and threshes a crop, usually corn.

Concentrates Granular or cubed barley mixed with minerals and other additives to form a concentrate livestock feed.

Continuous flow Any material handling which is continuous, usually including one specific activity, particularly with reference to a continuous-flow corn drier.

Controlled environment Livestock housing or crop storage in which the internal environment is controlled usually by electrically powered fans, heaters, coolers, etc.

Conveyor Mechanical equipment for conveying materials, usually referring to endless belt systems.

Corn The seed or grain of a cereal crop, usually related to the principal crop within a region (e.g. maize in the US, wheat in the UK), but it can be used for all the cereals grown in a locality.

Corral A fenced enclosure to pen cattle or sheep.

Court A northern term for an open cattle yard, possibly including some covered shelter.

Cowhouse A general term for dairy cattle housing, usually specific to those where cows are tied in stalls in rows between circulation and work passages.

Cowshed Usually synonymous with cowhouse.

Crate A pen for holding livestock, usually pigs, in which they cannot turn round and used for a specific period, such as farrowing, or sometimes permanently.

Creep A penned area into which youngstock have access, via openings too small for the adults, so that they can creep into a warmer, protected enclosure.

Crush A special pen for confining livestock individually, usually for veterinary inspection of cattle or for mating.

Crusher A device for crushing corn to create a meal.

Cubicle A railed stall for individual cattle, set in rows, but where the cattle are free to enter and leave the stall.

Cutter-bar The long, toothed bar which acts as the cutting mechanism on a combine harvester.

Dairy The room in which milk is cooled and stored, sometimes in which butter or cheese is processed. Dairy can be an adjective to both cow and farm to indicate specialization in milk production.

Deep litter Livestock bedding which is spread over old litter for periods of several months, thus creating farmyard manure which, later, can be spread as a fertilizer (see Bedded yard). Can also mean the droppings through a perforated floor in poultry housing.

Digester A tank in which effluent or dung is stored whilst anaerobic action breaks down the matter and releases methane gas.

Dip A horizontal tank, specially dimensioned, into which sheep can be dipped to cleanse their wool.

Doocot A Scottish term for Dovecote.

Dovecote A building for doves or pigeons to roost or breed, usually circular or square in plan. Many are medieval in origin.

Drier A container through which air can be blown to reduce the moisture in grain.

Dry sow A sow during the period following lactation, sometimes provided with a special building.

Dump box A container into which harvested grass can be dumped and from which a conveyor takes it to a place for storage.

Dung Livestock excreta, usually that used as a fertilizer. Can be used in conjunction with area (special areas for pigs in which to dung away from their bedding), heap (usually a form of midden), or hill (a mound of dung).

Dutch barn A steel-framed, curved-roofed barn for storing hay or straw bales, usually open sided, and based on the eighteenth-century timber barns in Holland.

Effluent The liquid waste from livestock, milk, silage or vegetable processing.

Electric dog A wire or pole, charged with low voltage, and which can be pulled to bring cattle forward, usually in a collecting yard to a parlour.

Elevator A mechanical device for lifting materials, usually a moving spiked belt for bales or roots.

Estate yard The enclosed yard for an estate to carry out general works, like a builders' yard.

Factory farm A farm which buys in rather than grows the feed for livestock, which may be permanently housed, and which is organized like a manufacturing industry.

Fallow Term applied to arable land left unploughed for a season or longer within a rotation.

Fank A Scottish term for a sheep house, originally for an outlying, fenced enclosure to provide protection.

Farmstead A farm complete with its buildings or steading.

Farmyard A yard within the steading which is protected from extreme exposure and usually guarded by the farmhouse.

Farrow Giving birth by a sow. Also applied to her litter.

Feed Food for livestock, usually referring to concentrates.

Feedlot A US term for extensive penning of livestock, usually beef cattle, for fattening and sometimes including 10,000 head on one site.

Fermentation A chemical change in stored crops, involving the production of sugar, acids and heat, generally to their detriment.

Finisher The last stages of fattening livestock. Can be used as an adjective to describe special yards or houses.

Flail A hinged pole used to thresh grain, but, in modern terms, can be equipment designed to lacerate grass after harvesting to improve it for silage.

Flax Two main-crop varieties, with a blue flower, used to produce linen fibre, or linseed oil, or cattle fodder.

Floating meadows A seventeenth-century method of irrigating grassland by harnessing and releasing river water through the topsoil.

Fodder Livestock food, usually the bulk roughages for cattle.

Fold An enclosed shelter, usually for sheep.

Follower The heifer which eventually follows into the milking herd.

Footbath A shallow, recessed area in a concrete floor, filled with dissolved medications, through which hooved livestock are taken to protect their feet from rot and other complaints.

Forage box A trailer, with an unloading device, used to distribute grass or chopped roots or other forage into cattle mangers.

Forearm loader The front attachment to a tractor and which can be used to lift, raise and place bulk materials, particularly crops or manure.

Gangway A passage for feeding or inspecting penned stock; a raised catwalk used for inspecting crops or stock.

Gilt A young sow, prior to mating; sometimes the adjective to a house or yard.

Gin-gang A building housing horse-powered machinery, with a drive shaft into an adjacent barn, usually circular or octagonal in plan.

Glasshouse A glazed building using solar energy to force crops.

Granary The storage building for corn, whether prior to or after threshing.

Greenhouse A synonym for glasshouse.

Grist The action of grinding corn, but can refer to the corn itself prior to being ground at a mill.

Hammer-mill Rotating hammers used to crush grain as a coarse feed.

Hay Mown grass stored in bales or loose for livestock feed, often either wilted or dried to reduce the moisture content.

Haylage Mown grass, wilted to under 50 per cent moisture content, and chopped for storage in a tower silo.

Hayrack A rack to hold hay from which it can be plucked by cattle.

Haystack The traditional method of stacking baled or loose hay for storage, usually with a thatched top, but now often sheeted in plastic.

Heavy hog Pigs fattened beyond bacon weight and up to 120–135 kilogrammes.

Heifer A young cow before her first lactation.

Helme A regional term for an implement shelter.

Herringbone parlour A milking parlour in which the cows stand obliquely to the operator's work pit so as to provide access to the udder.

Homestead A farmstead, specifically one including a family home.

Horrea A semi-open storage barn, based on Roman principles, for unthreshed corn, which permits drying winds to ventilate it.

Horse-mill A mill operated from a drive shaft turned by one or more horses, usually working within a gin-gang type of structure.

Intake pit A pit into which corn is tipped and from which it is elevated and conveyed into storage bins.

Intensive housing Stock housed with minimum or low spatial standards, often with automated equipment for feeding and cleaning and with controlled environments.

Jog-through A vibrating belt in a trough which jogs fodder along a manger.

Kennel A cubicle for cattle or pigs, but of cheap construction and usually of monopitch design and partially open.

Kibbler A mill which bruises and crushes grain coarsely.

Kiln A crop drying area in which warm air circulates via a plenum chamber through the crop.

Lagoon A compound or reservoir in which to store slurry.

Layer house A building to house a laying flock, usually hens.

Lean-to A structure acting as a lean-to roof against another building's wall or eaves.

Leat A watercourse or channel used to take a stream to a watermill.

Loft A storage area at an upper level in a building, usually for holding feed above livestock.

Longhouse A traditional, upland dwelling in which the farm buildings and house are in line and under one ridge.

Loosebox A box or stable for housing cattle or horses individually and untied.

Loosehouse A building to house livestock, particularly cattle, without them being tied.

Lucam A projection from a mill roof or gable, through the floor of which sacks may be hoisted from external ground-level or cart.

Manger A trough in which feed for livestock is placed, traditionally at each stall, but today often linear for groups of livestock penned or yarded together.

Mattress A rubber pad used as a bed for cattle stalls or cubicles.

Meal Finely ground grain used as a feed, often in concentrate form.

Mew A stable or loosebox, usually in an outbuilding.

Midden The place for dung taken from buildings, traditionally placed adjacent to a farmyard.

Midstrey The high-doored, cross opening and passage through a barn capable of taking corn wagons. During winter, corn was flailed in the midstrey.

Milking parlour A building or room containing equipment and stalls where cows are milked in batches from a central work-pit or area.

Milking point The position at which the cow is milked.

Milking unit The cluster and equipment used to milk cows in the parlour.

Milk pail The receptacle into which milk is taken from the cow by hand.

Mill The mechanism for grinding corn but often referring to the enclosing building for the operation of milling, sometimes coupled to its power source, whether horse, water or wind.

Mill-ging Horse-operated milling machinery, as gin-gang.

Mill-mix Plant to both mill grain and mix it with additives, forming a balanced concentrate feed.

Mixed farm A farm with both arable and livestock enterprises.

Model farm A farm, with buildings, organized and equipped to the highest standard, particularly referring to eighteenth- and nineteenth-century estate farms designed as showplaces.

Mow A passage in which either hay or grain is spread from a cart and to which cattle have access after it is deposited.

Muck A general term for manure.

Nest Square grain-storage bins of galvanized steel, bolted together with shared walls.

Oast A traditional hop drying kiln.

Open field Medieval fields with unfenced cultivation strips.

Organic farm A farm using livestock wastes and not chemical fertilizers.

Overshot wheel A watermill powered by water from a leat taken over the top of the waterwheel.

Package deal A building designed, supplied and erected by a manufacturer as a single contract.

Packhouse A building in which vegetable or fruit is packed for market or sale.

Paddock A small field used for grazing, usually near the farmstead. A field divided by temporary electric fencing to provide rotational plots or paddocks for grazing.

Pen A fenced or walled enclosure to contain livestock either in the field or in the building.

Pipeline A pipe, usually of stainless steel, to convey milk from a cow to a bulk tank.

Pit A sunken work area, especially in a milking parlour or vehicle workshop.

Pitchfork The traditional two-pronged fork used to lift bales and to pitch them on to a stack or into a yard.

Poach To overtread grassland so that it becomes a muddy patch.

Pophole A small hole in a wall for small livestock, particularly pigs, to pop through from pen to yard.

Post mill A windmill in which the upper part can turn around a post into the wind direction.

Precleaner Equipment to remove trash from incoming corn before it is more finely dressed and dried.

Press Equipment used to press a material to remove liquid.

Prime mover Powered equipment, from an intake of fuel, which may also be used to drive secondary machinery.

Pulsator An engine creating alternative pressure and suction and used to form a pulsating vacuum in the milking cluster.

Race A narrow fenced passage through which livestock are taken head to tail to permit individual attention, usually at a yoke or weigh crate.

Reception pit As for Intake pit.

Recording jar A jar through which extracted milk passes in order for its quantity to be recorded before it reached a dairy.

Rick A stack of hay or corn, originally thatched.

Rick yard An area on which several ricks were built, not necessarily as a yard.

Roller mill A mill which crushes grain between rollers.

Rotation A planned sequence of different crops in a field, usually taken in three or four year cycles.

Rotary A milking parlour in which the stalls rotate around the work pit.

Roughage An essential part of cattle diet, containing coarse fibre.

Ruakura crate A hinged, tubular farrowing crate, first developed in New Zealand.

Rubrail A rail at chest or body level against which cows can rub without touching the wall.

Rumprail A rail at tail level, especially that holding cows in a herring-bone parlour away from the pit.

Self-feeder A feeding hopper from which livestock can extract as much feed as they need.

Self-unloading trailer A trailer with an unloading device, particularly for grass or silage which is placed along a manger.

Separator Equipment which can separate two constituent parts of a material, such as cream from milk, or liquid from solid effluent.

Sheaf A bound bundle of unthreshed corn.

Shedder A pen into which an animal can be shed away from the herd or flock.

Shippon A regional term for a cowshed.

Sickle A curved blade on a handle used to cut corn.

Silage Abbreviated from ensilage, that is cut and possibly wilted grass conserved *en masse* by compaction and fermentation with reduced oxygen supply.

Silo A container holding a crop, particularly grain or grass.

Silobarn A barn with retaining walls used to hold silage.

Slat A floor for livestock made up with slats and spaces to suit their hooves, but allowing effluent to pass into a channel or pit below.

Slurry A dilute effluent, usually with under 10 per cent solid matter.

Smock mill A windmill with wall batter or taper walls, like a cone.

Solari house A farrowing-cum-fattening pen, with monopitch roof and open tall end, originally designed by Solari.

Sowstall A special stall to hold a sow, for a specific period of her cycle, whether dry or farrowing.

Space boards A wall of vertical boarding, set with small spaces between each board to provide ventilation for stock buildings.

Stable A fitted room in a building, designed for a horse.

Stack yard A rick yard.

Staddle A stone, shaped as a cone with a cap, on which a rick or granary is erected, designed so that rodents cannot climb to the crop.

Stall A partition area in a stock building to hold an animal.

Steading A settlement of farm buildings which service one farm.

Steer A young beef animal, especially if castrated.

Stell A Highland circular enclosure to provide shelter for sheep.

Stock A farm is stocked with dead or live purchases for its operation: normally stock refers to livestock.

Stones A pair of horizontal, circular stones, the upper one rotating, used to grind corn in a mill.

Stook A group of sheaves, stacked together in a field, to permit air-drying.

Sty A small pen or structure for pigs, usually in association with an open yard.

Surface cooler A stainless steel, hollow surface, chilled internally with cold water, over which milk trickles to reduce its body temperature to that acceptable for holding in a churn.

Swathe The extent of crop cut in one pass; with modern grass or straw cutting, essentially the linear width of cut crop as it lies.

Tandem A milking parlour in which the stalls are parallel at each side of the pit, but with a passage outside the stalls to permit each to be entered or exited separately.

Thresh To thrash corn until the grain is separated from the straw.

Tithe barn A granary in which the church's tithe was stored.

Tombstone A barrier of vertical baulks of timber, like tombstones, set 250 millimetres apart, but over which a cow can reach at prescribed spaces to drop her neck to reach fodder at the other side on the ground.

Tower mill A windmill set within a brick tower.

Tower silo A vertical silo used to conserve grass, made from prefabricated panels of galvanized steel, glass-fused steel or concrete staves, though early versions were of *in situ* concrete.

Tray drier A large perforated tray, holding grain in batches, through which air is blown to dry the grain.

Treadwheel A wheel turned by treading inside its rim and used to power machinery.

Tribulum A Roman floor used for threshing.

Tripod A structure of bound stakes, in a cone, over which mown grass is placed to air dry it for hay.

Trough A shaped manger for feeding livestock.

Umbrella A wide-span, general-purpose building in which the roof acts as an umbrella for several unspecific tasks.

Undershot wheel A watermill powered by water from a leat taken underneath the waterwheel.

Unit The organization of a farm enterprise as a single, productive unit.

Vacuum tanker A tractor-powered tanker used to hold liquids, particularly effluents, and filled by suction under vacuum.

Warehouse A building to store ware, that is edible (as opposed to seed) potatoes.

Water-wheel A wheel, turned by water power, used to drive machinery, particularly that in a watermill.

Weaner house A building in which weaned piglets reach about 25 kilograms in weight.

Weigh crate A crate designed for weighing individual or batches of livestock.

Wheelhouse A structure in which an animal-powered wheel operates; a gin-gang.

Whey Milk from which most of the fat content has been extracted, often used to feed pigs.

Whole-crop A crop harvested with seed still on the stalk, whether grass or grain.

Wilt To permit a cut crop to dry out on the ground before harvesting, particularly grass for hay or silage.

Winnow To allow an air current to remove dust from threshed grain.

Winter house Livestock buildings used specifically during winter months.

Woolroom The room in which fleeces are stored after clipping.

Yard A fenced or walled enclosure for livestock, sometimes roofed.

Yard-and-parlour Cattle housing in yards combined with an adjacent milking parlour.

Yoke A barrier which also holds an animal by the neck, used both for individual feeding and for temporary inspection.

Yorkshire boarding A roof of grooved timber boards, from ridge to eaves, with air spaces between for livestock house ventilation.

Zero graze Grass cut by machine and fed to cattle away from the fields, usually at the steading, so that there is no grazing.

Chronological Development of Modern Food Production to 1920

c.1660 simple horse-mills
1701 Jethro Tull's seed-drill
1720 James Meikle's winnowing machine
c.1750 evolution of nationally known implements and works began
1760 simple chaff-cutter
1770 spiral knife chaff-cutter
1771 Arbuthnot's mould-board plough
1774 first threshing machine
1782 James Cooke's drill (ancestor to modern drill)
1786 Andrew Meikle's thresher (first successful)
1794 James Cooke's chaff-cutter (ancestor to modern cutter)
1798 John Wilkinson's steam thresher
c.1800 development of rick yard instead of barn
1800 Joseph Boyce's reaper
1800 root-cutter
c.1810 ricks erected on wheeled platforms on tracks
1811 Appert's tin-plate canisters for food
1814 vegetable soups and preserved meats used by Royal Navy
1815 greenhouses with cast-iron framed sash-bars
c.1825 livestock slatted floors
1826 Patrick Bell's reaper (first successful)
1830 rotary root-cutter
1833 steam plough
1840 horse-powered overhead shafting to barn machinery
1851 impetus of Great Exhibition to all farm machinery and mass production
1855 first patent in England for dried milk
c.1860 mechanical milking by vacuum
c.1860 milk transported by railways to towns
c.1860 corrugated-iron sheeting as rick covers
c.1865 first milk cooler on farm
c.1865 portable steam thresher used in fields
c.1875 corrugated-iron framed Dutch barn
1877 Gustav de Laval centrifugal cream-separator (Sweden)
c.1880 gas-powered barn machinery

c.1885 lighting from methane gas from livestock
  1889 gasoline-engine tractor
  1902 power-take-off from tractor engine
c.1905 electrical power in the barn
  1922 Hosier's portable milking bail

Bibliography

I. H. Adams, *Agrarian Landscape Farms—A Glossary for Historical Geography*. Institute of British Geography, 1976

G. H. Andrews, *Rudimentary Treatise on Agricultural Engineering*, Vol. 1, *Buildings*; Vol. 2, *Motive Power* (on machinery of the Steading), London, 1852

J. Apps and A. Strang, *Barns of Wisconsin*, Tamarack Press, Wisconsin, 1977

J. Arnold, *Farm Wagons of England and Wales*, John Barker, 1969

J. Arnold, *Farm Wagons and Carts*, David & Charles, 1977

E. Arthur and D. Witney, *The Barn—A Vanishing Landmark in North America*, McClelland & Stewart, Toronto, 1972

M. S. Barley, *The English Farmhouse and Cottage*, Routledge & Kegan Paul, 1961

H. J. Barre and L. L. Sammet, *Farm Structures*, J. Wiley, 1950

E. Beaton, *Doocots of Caithness*, Scottish Vernacular Buildings Group, 1980

E. Beaton, *Doocots of Moray*, Moray Field Club, 1978

A. Beaumont, *Ransomes Steam Engines*, David & Charles, 1972

Berger-Levrault (Ed.), *L'Architecture Rurale Française*, Musée National des Arts et Traditions Populaires, Paris, 1979

Biffoli, *La Case Colonica in Toscana*, Vallecchi, 1966

Board of Agriculture, *Communications to the Board of Agriculture on Farm Buildings*, London, 1796

J. R. Bond, *Farm Implements and Machinery*, Benn, 1923

H. Bonnett, *Saga of the Steam Plough*, David & Charles, 1972

H. Bonnett, *Farming with Steam*, Shire Publications, 1974

M. S. Briggs, *The English Farmhouse*, Batsford, 1963

R. E. Brown, *Book of the Landed Estate*, London, 1869

H. Brunner, 'Circular Horse Power—the Rotary Animal Engine', *Country Life*, 2 March 1978, pp. 557–9

H. Brunner and J. K. Major, 'Water Raising by Animal Power', *Journal of the Hist. of Ind. and Tech.*, Vol. 9, No. 2, May 1972, pp. 117–51

R. W. Brunskill, *Illustrated Handbook of Vernacular Architecture*, Faber, 1970; 2nd edition 1978

J. F. Burke, *British Husbandry*, Society for the Diffusion of Useful Knowledge, London, 1834–40

D. G. Carter, *Farm Buildings*, J. Wiley, 1922

C. L. Cawood, 'The History and Development of Farm Tractors', *Journal of the Hist. of Ind. and Tech.*, Vol. 7, No. 3, and No. 4, August 1970 and November 1970

R. A. Chambers, 'A Deserted Mediaeval Farmstead at Sadler's Wood, Lewknor', Oxoniensia, Vol. XXXVIII, 1973, pp. 146–67

S. D. Chapman and J. D. Chambers, The Beginnings of the Industrial Revolution, Ch. V 'Agriculture and the Supply of Food', University Tutorial Press, 1970

K. Chivers, The Shire Horse—A History of the Breed, the Society and the Men, J. A. Allen, 1976

M. S. Clark, Development of farm buildings in Scotland with particular reference to Angus, Thesis, Scott Sutherland School of Architecture, Aberdeen, 1976

A. D. Clarke, Modern Farm Buildings, London, 1891

R. Cockrill, The Buffaloes of China, Food and Agriculture Organisation, HMSO, London, 1976

E. J. T. Collins, From Sickle to Combine, Museum of English Rural Life, Reading, 1970

M. and R. Conrat, The American Farm—A Photographic History, Scolar Press, 1977

S. Copeland, Agriculture, Ancient and Modern, London, 1866

Cords-Parchim, Das Handbuch des Landbau-meisters, Neumann Verlag, 1952

H. Cox, Silo for Preserving British Fodder Crops Stored in a Green State, Strand, London, 1885

J. S. Creasey, The Draught Ox, Institute of Agricultural History, Reading, 1974

C. Culpin, Farm Machinery, Crosby Lockwood Staples, 9th ed., 1976 (1938)

G. Darlay, The National Trust Book of the Farm, Weidenfeld & Nicolson, 1981

T. Davis, John Fowler and the Business he Founded, privately printed, 1951

J. B. Denton, Farm Homesteads of England, London, 1863

J. Ewart, Treatise on the Arrangement and Construction of Agricultural Buildings, London, 1851

K. Falconer, Guide to England's Industrial Heritage, Batsford, 1980

A. Fenton, 'Draught Oxen in Britain', Bull. D'Ethnographie Tchecoslovaque, 1969

A. Fenton, Farming township –Auchindrain, Countryside Commission for Scotland, 1979

A. Fenton, The Island Blackhouse, HMSO, London, 1978

H. Fillipetti and J. Trotereau, Symboles et Pratiques Rituelles dans la maison paysanne traditionnelle, 1978

B. J. Finch, Ploughing Engines at Work, Percival Marshall, 1962

J. Fitchen, The New World Dutch Barn, Syracuse University Press, 1968

N. E. Fox, 'The Spread of the Threshing Machine in Central Southern England', Agric. Hist. Rev., Vol. 26, Pt. 1, 1978, pp. 26–8

C. Fraser, *Harry Ferguson—Inventor and Pioneer*, John Murray, 1972

J. Friel, *L'Architecture Paysanne*, Paris, 1977

G. E. Fussell, *The Farmers' Tools 1500–1900*, Melrose, 1952

G. E. Fussell, *Farming Technique from Prehistoric to Modern Times*, Pergamon Press, 1966

G. E. Fussell, *The Classical Tradition in West European Farming*, David & Charles, 1972

G. E. Fussell, *Jethro Tull—his Influence on Mechanised Agriculture*, Osprey, 1973

A. Gailey and A. Fenton, *The Spade in Northern and Atlantic Europe*, Ulster Folk Museum, 1970

J. Gandy, *The Rural Architect*, London, 1805

D. R. Grace and D. C. Phillips, *Ransomes of Ipswich—A History of the Firm and Guide to its Records*, Institute of Agricultural History, 1975

W. J. Grime, *The Highland vernacular*, Thesis, Scott Sutherland School of Architecture, Aberdeen, 1978

J. E. Grundy, 'Outline of the Development of Stone Barns in East Lancashire', *Vernacular Architecture*, Vernacular Architecture Group, 1976

Sir R. de Zouche Hall (Ed.), *A Bibliography of Vernacular Architecture*, David & Charles, 1972

B. D. Halsted, *Barns, Sheds and Outbuildings*, S. Greene, Vermont, 1977

A. G. Harris, T. B. Muckle and J. A. Shaw, *Farm Machinery*, OUP, 1970

R. Harris, *Traditional Farm Buildings—A Catalogue to Accompany the Touring Exhibition*, Arts Council of Great Britain, London, 1978

N. Harvey, *A History of Farm Buildings in England and Wales*, David & Charles, 1970

N. Harvey, *Old Farm Buildings*, Shire Publications, 1975

N. Harvey, *Fields, Hedges and Ditches*, Shire Publications, 1976

N. Harvey, *Farms and Farming*, Shire Publications, 1977

N. Harvey, *Industrial Archaeology of Farming in England and Wales*, Batsford, 1980

R. Henderson, *The Modern Farmstead*, London, 1902

T. Hennell, *Change on the Farm*, CUP, 1934

I. Homes, 'The Agricultural Use of the Herefordshire House and its Outbuildings', *Vernacular Architecture*, Vernacular Architecture Group, Vol. 9, pp. 12–16, 1978

K. Hooker and M. Hunt, *Farmhouses and Small Provincial Buildings in Southern Italy*, Architectural Book Publishing Co., NY, 1925

W. J. Hughes, *A Century of Traction Engines*, Pan, 1972

K. Hutton, 'The Distribution of Wheelhouses in the British Isles', *Agric. Hist. Rev.*, Vol. 24, Pt. 1, pp. 30–5, 1976

M. G. Jarrett and S. Wrathmell, '16th–17th Century Farmsteads, West Whelpington, Northumberland', *Agric. Hist. Rev.*, Vol. 25, Pt. 11, pp. 108–19, 1977

J. G. Jenkins, *The English Farm Wagon*, David & Charles, 1972

C. A. Jewell, *Victorian Farming* (from *The Book of the Farm*, Henry Stephens, 1844), Barry Shurlock, 1975

I. Jones, *Historic Farms of the Wine Route in South Africa*, Vernacular Architecture Society of South Africa, No. 1, 1975

T. Keegan, *The Heavy Horse—its Harness and Decoration*, Pelham, 1973

Kenji, *Architecture of the Japanese Farming Community*, private volume, RIBA Library, 1976

E. Kerridge, *The Farmers of Old England*, Allen & Unwin, 1973

E. E. Kimbell, *The Compleat Traction Engineman*, Ian Allen, 1972

A. Kotsis, *Farm Buildings (Designs)*, Egyetemi Nyomda, Budapest, 1947

M. R. Lane, *The Story of the Steam Plough Works of John Fowler at Leeds*, Northgate, 1979

W. H. Long, 'The development of mechanization in English farming', *Ag. Hist. Rev.*, Vol. XI, 1963, pp. 15–26

J. C. Loudon, *Encyclopaedia of Cottage, Farm and Villa Architecture*, London, 1833

D. Low, *On Landed Property*, London, 1844

R. Lugar, *The Country Gentleman's Architect*, London, 1807 (reprint, Gregg, 1971)

S. Macdonald, 'The Progress of the Early Threshing Machine', *Agric. Hist. Rev.*, Vol. 23, Pt. 1, pp. 63–77, 1975

S. Macdonald, 'Further Progress with the Early Threshing Machine', *Agric. Hist. Rev.*, Vol. 26, Pt. 1, pp. 29–32, 1975

D. H. McHardy, *Modern Farm Buildings*, London, 1932

W. J. Maldon, *Farm Buildings*, London, 1896

G. I. Merion-Jones, 'The Longhouse—A Definition', *Jnl. of Med. Archaeol.*, 1973

R. S. Morton, *Traditional Farm Architecture in Scotland*, Ramsay Head Press, 1976

Helmut Ottenjann and Helmut Tecklenburg, *Alte Bauernhäuser zwischen Wases und Ems*, Museumsdorf Cloppenburg, 1979

R. A. C. Parker, *Coke of Norfolk—A Financial and Agricultural Study 1707–1842*, OUP, 1975

M. Partridge, *Farm Tools Through the Ages*, Osprey, 1973

J. B. Passmore, *The English Plough*, OUP, 1930

J. E. C. Peters, *The Development of Farm Buildings of Western Lowland Staffordshire up to 1880*, Manchester UP, 1969

J. E. C. Peters, *Discovering Traditional Farmbuilding*, Shire Publications, 1981

P. Peters, *Umbau alter Bauernhäuser*, München, 1978

J. Plaw, *Rural Architecture (Houses)*, London, 1802

J. A. Ransome, *The Implements of Agriculture*, J. Ridgeway, 1843

J. Reynolds, *Windmills and Watermills*, Hugh Evelyn, 1970

G. Rickman, *Roman Granaries and Store Buildings*, CUP, 1971

J. M. Robinson, 'Estate Buildings at Holkham', *Country Life*, 21 November 1974, pp. 1554–6; 28 November 1974, pp. 1642–5

J. M. Robinson, 'Estate Buildings of the Fifth and Sixth Dukes of Bedford at Woburn 1787–1839', *Arch. Rev.*, November 1976, pp. 276–81

J. M. Robinson, 'Model Farm Buildings of the Age of Improvement', *Agric. Hist. Jnl.*, Vol. 19, 1976, pp. 17–30

L. T. C. Rolt, *Waterloo Ironworks—A History of Taskers of Andover 1809–1968*, David & Charles, 1969

J. J. Rossiter, *Roman Farm Buildings in Italy*, BAR International Series, No. 52, Oxford, 1978

A. Roussell, 'Farms and Churches of the Mediaeval Norse Settlements of Greenland', *Reitzels Forlag*, Copenhagen, 1941

R. Samuel, *Village Life and Labour*, History Workshop Series, Routledge & Kegan Paul, 1975

R. B. Sayce, 'Farm Buildings', *Estates Gazette*, 1966

J. Scott, *Farm Buildings*, London, 1884

Scottish Vernacular Buildings Working Group, 'Building construction in Scotland – some historical and regional aspects', Report of Conference, Edinburgh, 1976

M. E. Seebohm, *The Evolution of the English Farm*, EP Publishing, 1976

H. A. Shearer, *Farm Buildings with Plans and Descriptions*, Chicago, 1917

J. M. Shippen and J. C. Turner, *Basic Farm Machinery*, Pergamon, 1970

A. L. Shoemaker, *The Pennsylvanian Barn*, Pennsylvania Dutch Folklore Centre, Franklin and Marshall College, 1955

C. Simonett, *Die Bauernhäuser des Kantons Graubünden*, Basel, 1965

J. Slight and R. S. Burn (Ed. H. Stephens), *The Book of Farm Implements and Machines*, Blackwood, 1858

E. Sloane, *American Barns and Covered Bridges*, W. Funk, NY, 1954

E. Sloane, *An Age of Barns*, Funk & Wagnalls, NY, 1967

C. C. Spence, *God Speed the Plow—The Coming of Steam Cultivation to Great Britain*, University of Illinois Press, 1976

J. Starforth, *Architecture of the Farm*, London, 1853

A. Steensberg, *Researches into Village Archaeology, Farms and Water Mills in Denmark during 2000 Years*, Copenhagen, 1952

A. Steensberg, A. Fenton and G. Lerche (Ed.), *Tools and Tillage*, Vol. 1, 1968–71; Vol. II, 1972–75; Vol. III, 1976–79, National Museum of Denmark, Copenhagen

H. Stephens and R. S. Burn, *The Book of Farm Buildings—Their Arrangement and Construction*, Blackwood, 1861

S. Taylor, *Modern Homesteads*, London, 1905

Viscount Torrington, *On Farm Buildings*, London, 1845

S. Toulson, *Discovering Farm Museums and Farm Parks*, Shire Publications, 1977

W. Tritton, 'The Origin of the Thrashing Machine', *Lincolnshire Magazine*, 1956, reprinted Soc. for Lincolnshire History and Archaeology, 1980

R. Trow-Smith, *Power on the Land*, Agripress Publicity, 1975

C. Tyler and J. Haining, *Ploughing by Steam—A History of Cultivation over the Years*, Model & Allied Publishers, 1970

C. Tyler, *Digging by Steam*, Argus, 1977

C. Tyler, *Ploughing by Steam*, Argus, 1977

J. Vince, *Discovering Carts and Wagons*, Shire Publications, 1970

J. Vince, *Farms and Farming*, Ian Allen, 1971

J. Vince, *Vintage Farm Machines*, Shire Publications, 1973

J. Vince, *Old Farm Tools*, Shire Publications, 1974

J. Vincent, *Country Cottages*, London, 1861

Vom Verbande Deutscher, *Das Bauernhaus in Deutsche Reiche und in seinen Grenzgebieten* (2 Vols), Dresden, 1906

G. Wainwright, 'A Celtic Farmstead in Southern Britain', *Scientific American*, December 1977, pp. 157–64

C. Waistrell, *Designs for Agricultural Buildings*, London, 1827

B. Walker, *Clay Buildings in North-East Scotland*, Scottish Vernacular Buildings Working Group, 1977

B. Walker, 'The Influence of Fixed Farm Machinery on Farm Building Design in East Scotland', *Archaeol. of Ind. Scotland*, 1977

M. Watney and S. Watney, *Horse Power*, Hamlyn, 1975

J. B. Weller, *Farm Buildings*, Vol. 1, Crosby Lockwood, 1965; *Farm Buildings*, Vol. 2, Crosby Lockwood Staples, 1972

J. B. Weller, *Modern Agriculture and Rural Planning*, Architectural Press, 1968

J. B. Weller, *Costruzioni Agricole e Zootechniche*, Edagricole, 1976

J. B. Weller, *Planning Farm Buildings*, Farm Buildings Information Centre, National Agricultural Centre, 1977

J. B. Weller (Ed.), *Coleshill Model Farm—Past, Present & Future*, RIBA, London, 1981

J. B. Weller, *Agricultural Buildings and Allied Controls*, Capital Planning Information, Edinburgh, 1981

J. B. Weller and S. Willetts, *Farm Wastes Management*, Crosby Lockwood Staples, 1977

K. D. White, *Agricultural Implements of the Roman World*, CUP, 1967

K. D. White, *Roman Farming*, Thames & Hudson, 1970

L. White, *Mediaeval Technology and Social Change*, OUP, 1962

R. A. Whitehead, *Garretts of Leiston*, Percival Marshall, 1964

R. A. Whitehead, *A Century of Service—An Illustrated History of Eddison Plant Ltd.*, Eddison Plant, 1968

R. A. Whitehead, *The Age of the Traction Engine*, Ian Allen, 1970

D. Wild, 'Conserving H. Haring's Cowshed', *Building Design*, 17 November, 1978, pp. 26–27

E. William, *Adeiladau Fferm traddodiadol yng Nghymru (Traditional Farm Buildings of Wales)*, Welsh Folk Museum, Cardiff, 1974

P. Wilkes, *An Illustrated History of Farming*, Spurbooks, 1978

E. H. D. Williams, 'Curing Chambers and Domestic Corn-drying Kilns', *Somerset Archaeol. and Nat. Hist. Soc.*, 1976

M. Williams, *Steam Power in Agriculture*, Blandford Press, 1977

Revd. J. M. Wilson, *The Rural Cyclopedia*, Edinburgh, 1847

T. Winder, *Handbook of Farm Buildings*, London 1908

J. Wood, *Plans of Cottages*, 1781

J. C. Wooley, *Planning Farm Buildings*, McGraw Hill, 1941

W. Wray, *Rural Architecture*, London, 1852

P. A. Wright, *Old Farm Implements*, A. & C. Black, 1961

P. A. Wright, *Old Farm Tractors*, A. & C. Black, 1962

P. A. Wright, *Salute the Carthorse*, Ian Allen, 1971

Chronological Bibliography

Principal Works on Farmsteads to 1914:

1774 T. Lightoler, *The Gentleman and Farmers' Architect*, London

1781 J. Wood, *Plans of Cottages*, London

1796 *Communications to the Board of Agriculture on Farm Buildings*, London

1796 R. Beaston, *On Farm Buildings*, London

1802 J. Plaw, *Rural Architecture*, London

1805 J. Gandy, *The Rural Architect*, London

1827 C. Waistrell, *Designs for Agricultural Buildings*, London

1830 P. F. Robinson, *Designs for Farm Buildings*, London

1833 J. C. Loudon, *Encyclopaedia of Cottage*, Farm and Villa

1844 D. Low, *On Landed Property*, London

1844 H. Stephens, *The Book of the Farm*, London

1845 Viscount Torrington, *On Farm Buildings*, London

1847 Revd. J. M. Wilson, *The Rural Cyclopedia*, Edinburgh

1851 J. Ewart, *Treatise on the Arrangement and Construction of Agricultural Buildings*, London

1852 G. H. Andrews, *Rudimentary Treatise on Agricultural Engineering*, Vol. 1, Buildings; Vol. 2, Motive Power, London

1853 J. Starforth, *Architecture of the Farm*, London

1858 J. Slight and R. S. Burn (Ed. H. Stephens), *The Book of Farm Implements and Machines*, Blackwood

1861 H. Stephens and R. S. Burn, *The Book of Farm Buildings—Their Arrangement and Construction*, Blackwood

1861 J. Vincent, *Country Cottages*, London

1863 J. B. Denton, *Farm Homesteads of England*, London

1866 S. Copeland, *Agriculture, Ancient and Modern*, London

1869 R. E. Brown, *Book of the Landed Estate*, London

1884 J. Scott, *Farm Buildings*, London

1891 A. D. Clarke, *Modern Farm Buildings*, London

1896 W. J. Maldon, *Farm Buildings*, London

1902 R. Henderson, *The Modern Farmstead*, London

1905 S. Taylor, *Modern Homesteads*, London

1908 T. Winder, *Handbook of Farm Buildings*, London

Index